Part I

Alternate Exercises and Problems

Alternate Exercises and Problems

for use with

Intermediate Accounting

Second Edition

J. David Spiceland
University of Memphis

James F. Sepe
Santa Clara University

Lawrence A. Tomassini
The Ohio State University

Prepared by
J. David Spiceland
James F. Sepe

Boston Burr Ridge, IL Dubuque, IA Madison, WI New York San Francisco St. Louis
Bangkok Bogotá Caracas Lisbon London Madrid
Mexico City Milan New Delhi Seoul Singapore Sydney Taipei Toronto

McGraw-Hill Higher Education

A Division of The ***McGraw-Hill*** *Companies*

Alternate Exercises and Problems for use with
INTERMEDIATE ACCOUNTING

1 2 3 4 5 6 7 8 9 0 QPD/QPD 0 9 8 7 6 5 4 3 2 1 0

ISBN 0-07-240497-3

http://www.mhhe.com

CONTENTS

Part I: Alternate Exercises and Problems

Chapter

Part II: Alternate Exercise and Problem Solutions

Chapter

Section 1

The Role of Accounting As an Information System

EXERCISES

Exercise 1-1
Accrual accounting

Listed below are several transactions that took place during the first two years of operations for the accounting firm of Haskins and Price.

	Year 1	**Year 2**
Amounts billed to customers for services rendered	$380,000	$440,000
Cash collected from customers	330,000	450,000
Cash disbursements:		
Payment of rent for two years	60,000	- 0 -
Salaries paid to employees for services rendered during the year	200,000	210,000
Travel	50,000	60,000
Utilities	30,000	50,000

In addition, you learn that the company incurred utility costs of $40,000 in year one, that there were no liabilities at the end of year two, and no anticipated bad debts on receivables.

Required:

1 Calculate the net operating cash flow for years 1 and 2.
2. Prepare an income statement for each year according to the accrual accounting model.
3. Determine the amount of receivables from customers that the company would show on its year 1 and year 2 balance sheets prepared according to the accrual accounting model.

Exercise 1-2
Concepts; terminology; conceptual framework

Listed below are several terms and phrases associated with the FASB's conceptual framework and underlying accounting principles. Pair each item from List A (by letter) with the item from List B that is most appropriately associated with it.

List A	List B
____ 1. predictive value	a. applying the same accounting practices over time
____ 2. relevance	b. record expenses in the period the related revenue is recognized
____ 3. reliability	c. concerns the relative size of an item and its effect on decisions
____ 4. comprehensive income	d. concerns the recognition of revenue
____ 5. materiality	e. along with relevance, a primary decision-specific quality
____ 6. consistency	f. the original transaction value upon acquisition
____ 7. verifiability	g. information is useful in predicting the future
____ 8. matching principle	h. pertinent to the decision at hand
____ 9. historical cost principle	i. implies consensus among different measurers
____10. realization principle	j. the change in equity from nonowner transactions

Exercise 1-3
Basic assumptions and principles

Listed below are several statements that relate to financial accounting and reporting. Identify the basic assumption, broad accounting principle, or pervasive constraint which applies to each statement.

1. IBM provides quarterly financial information to its shareholders.
2. Cisco Corporation amortizes the cost of a patent over the patent's useful life.
3. The Zilog Company depreciates the cost of its equipment rather than the current fair market value of the equipment.
4. The Antiel Corporation included a disclosure note describing a lawsuit it is defending even though the suit has not yet been settled.
5. The Feinstein Corporation records revenue when products are delivered to customers, even though the cash has not yet been received.
6. John Gordon, the sole proprietor of Gordon's Hardware, does not list his personal automobile on the balance sheet of the hardware store.

Exercise 1-4
Basic assumptions and principles

Identify the basic assumption or broad accounting principle that was violated in each of the following situations.

1. Don Sherwood, a shareholder of the Brady Construction Corporation, has not received a financial statement from the company for over two years.
2. The Diatonics Corporation reported equipment on its balance sheet at fair market value.
3. Holyoke Corporation paid $20,000 for a three-year insurance policy and recorded the entire expenditure as insurance expense.
4. The Acme Appliance Company is involved in a major lawsuit. The company is being sued for $10 million dollars for alleged patent infringement. The company believes the suit is without merit and has not disclosed its existence in its financial statements.
5. The Ravel Company's balance sheet includes assets owned by the company as well as assets of its principal shareholder, Jim Thomas.
6. The Marine Chemical Company recorded revenue for a $50,000 advance payment received from a customer. The customer's order will be shipped next month.

EXERCISES

Exercise 2-1
Transaction analysis

The following transactions occurred during April 2000, for the Unisale Corporation. The company owns and operates a wholesale warehouse.

1. Issued 100,000 shares of capital stock in exchange for $800,000 in cash.
2. Purchased equipment at a cost of $60,000. $15,000 cash was paid and a note payable was signed for the balance owed.
3. Purchased inventory on account at a cost of $270,000. The company uses the perpetual inventory system.
4. Credit sales for the month totaled $360,000. The cost of the goods sold was $210,000.
5. Paid $20,000 in rent on the warehouse building for the month of April.
6. Paid $15,000 to an insurance company for comprehensive insurance for a two-year period beginning May 1, 2000.
7. Paid $180,000 on account for the merchandise purchased in 3.
8. Collected $190,000 from customers on account.
9. Recorded depreciation expense of $2,000 for the month on the equipment.

Required:

Analyze each transaction and show the effect of each on the accounting equation for a corporation.

Example:

	Assets	=	Liabilities	+	Paid-in Capital	+	Retained Earnings
1.	+800,000(Cash)				+800,000(Capital stock)		

Exercise 2-2
Journal entries

Prepare general journal entries to record each of the transactions listed in Exercise 2-1.

Exercise 2-3
Debits and credits

Indicate whether a credit will increase (I) or decrease (D) each of the following accounts:

	Increase (I) or Decrease (D)	Account
1.	______	Accounts receivable
2.	______	Salary expense
3.	______	Loss on sale of land
4.	______	Prepaid insurance
5.	______	Interest revenue
6.	______	Capital stock
7.	______	Interest payable
8.	______	Land
9.	______	Interest expense
10.	______	Gain on sale of equipment
11.	______	Interest expense
12.	______	Accumulated depreciation
13.	______	Bad debt expense
14.	______	Sales revenue

Exercise 2-4
Transaction analysis; debits and credits

Some of the ledger accounts for the Southern Lumber Company are numbered and listed below. For each of the November 2000 transactions numbered 1 through 12 below, indicate by account number which accounts should be debited and credited. The company uses the perpetual inventory system. Assume that appropriate adjusting entries were made at the end of October.

(1) Accounts payable	(2) Equipment	(3) Inventory
(4) Accounts receivable	(5) Cash	(6) Supplies
(7) Supplies expense	(8) Prepaid insurance	(9) Sales revenue
(10) Retained earnings	(11) Note payable	(12) Capital stock
(13) Interest payable	(14) Rent expense	(15) Wages payable
(16) Cost of goods sold	(17) Wage expense	(18) Interest expense

	Account(s) Debited	Account(s) Credited
Example: Purchased equipment for cash	2	5
1. Paid a cash dividend.		
2. Paid insurance for the next six months.		
3. Sold goods to customers on account.		
4. Purchased inventory for cash.		
5. Purchased supplies on account.		
6. Paid employees wages for November.		
7. Issued capital stock in exchange for cash.		
8. Collected cash from customers on account		
9. Borrowed cash from a bank and signed a note.		
10. At the end of November, recorded the amount of supplies that had been used during the month.		
11. Paid October's interest on a bank loan.		
12. Accrued interest expense for November.		

Exercise 2-5
Adjusting entries

Prepare the necessary adjusting entries at December 31, 2000, for the Jasper Company for each of the following situations. Assume that no financial statements were prepared during the year and no adjusting entries were recorded.

1. A two-year fire insurance policy was purchased on August 1, 2000, for $12,000. The company debited prepaid insurance for the entire amount.
2. Depreciation on equipment totaled $20,000 for the year.
3. Employee salaries of $27,000 for the month of December will be paid in early January, 2001.
4. On October 1, 2000, the company lent $50,000 to a customer. The customer signed a note that requires principal and interest at 8% to be paid on September 30, 2001.
5. In July, the company purchased supplies for $4,500. The entry was recorded as a debit to supplies expense. Supplies on hand at the end of the year totaled $2,200. No supplies had been previously purchased.

Exercise 2-6
Cash versus accrual accounting; adjusting entries

The Calloway Tennis Ball Company prepares monthly financial statements for its bank. The November 30 and December 31, 2000, balance sheets contained the following account information:

	Nov. 30		Dec. 31	
	Dr.	Cr.	Dr.	Cr.
Supplies	4,000		8,000	
Prepaid rent	10,000		7,000	
Interest payable		7,000		4,000
Unearned rent revenue		4,500		3,000

The following information also is known:

a. The December statement of cash flows reported $6,000 in cash paid for supplies.
b. No rent payments were made in December.
c. The December income statement revealed $2,000 in interest expense.
d. On November 1, 2000, a tenant paid Calloway $6,000 in advance rent for the period November through February. Unearned rent revenue was credited.

Required:

1. What was the amount of supplies expense that appeared in the December income statement?
2. What was the amount of rent expense that appeared in the December income statement?
3. What was the amount of cash paid to the company's creditors for interest during December?
4. What was the amount of rent revenue earned in December? What adjusting entry was recorded at the end of December for unearned rent?

PROBLEMS

Problem 2-1
Accounting cycle through unadjusted trial balance

The Tazmanian Hat Company began business in July, 1998. During July, the following transactions occurred:

Jul. 1 Issued capital stock in exchange for $1,000,000 cash.
2 Purchased inventory on account for $80,000 (the perpetual inventory system is used).
4 Paid the company's landlord $10,000 for rent for the upcoming year.
10 Sold merchandise on account for $120,000. The cost of the merchandise was $75,000.
15 Borrowed $ 50,000 from a local bank and signed a note. Principal and interest at 10% is to be repaid in one year.
20 Paid employees $15,000 wages for the first half of the month.
24 Paid $50,000 to suppliers for the merchandise purchased on July 2.
26 Collected $60,000 on account from customers.
28 Paid various utility bills of $1,500 for the month of July.
31 Paid $8,000 in insurance for the period August 1, 2000 to October 1, 2000.

Required:

1. Prepare general journal entries to record each transaction. Omit explanations.
2. Post the entries to T-accounts.
3. Prepare an unadjusted trial balance as of July 31, 2000.

Problem 2-2
Adjusting entries

The Salem Bread Company produces and sells various bakery products to restaurants. The company's fiscal year-end is December 31. The unadjusted trial balance as of December 31, 2000, appears below.

Account Title	Debits	Credits
Cash	32,000	
Accounts receivable	85,000	
Prepaid rent	4,000	
Supplies	2,300	
Inventory	80,000	
Equipment	225,000	
Accumulated depreciation - equipment		77,000
Accounts payable		38,000
Wages payable		5,000
Note payable		50,000
Interest payable		- 0 -
Unearned revenue		3,000
Capital stock		100,000
Retained earnings		127,300
Sales revenue		256,000
Cost of goods sold	145,000	
Wage expense	62,000	
Rent expense	10,000	
Depreciation expense	- 0 -	
Interest expense	- 0 -	
Supplies expense	3,000	
Miscellaneous expense	8,000	
Totals	656,300	656,300

Information necessary to prepare the year-end adjusting entries appears below.

1. Depreciation on the equipment for the year is $22,000.
2. Wages payable at the end of the month should be $7,000.
3. On April 1, 2000, Salem borrowed $50,000 from a local bank and signed a note. The note requires interest to be paid annually on March 31 at 8%. The principal is due in 5 years.
4. $1,000 of supplies remained on hand at December 31, 2000.
5. In November, a customer paid Salem $3,000 for an order that was delivered in December. The cash received was credited to Unearned revenue. No other customer advances were received during the year.
6. On December 1, 2000, $4,000 rent was paid to the owner of the building. The payment represented rent for December through March 2001, at $1,000 per month.

Required:
Prepare the necessary December 31, 2000, adjusting journal entries.

EXERCISES

Exercise 3-1
Income statement format; single-step and multiple-step

The following is a partial trial balance for Apex Computer Corporation as of December 31, 2000:

Account Title	Debits	Credits
Sales revenue		3,400,000
Interest revenue		35,000
Gain on sale of equipment		30,000
Loss from hurricane damage (event is both unusual and infrequent)	300,000	
Cost of goods sold	2,250,000	
Restructuring costs	400,000	
Administrative expense	450,000	
Selling expense	150,000	
Interest expense	20,000	

500,000 shares of common stock were outstanding throughout 2000. Income tax expense has not yet been accrued. The income tax rate is 40%.

Required:
1. Prepare a single-step income statement for 2000, including EPS disclosure.
2. Prepare a multiple-step income statement for 2000, including EPS disclosure.

Exercise 3-2
Discontinued operations

The Bilibong Company had three distinct operating divisions. The sports equipment division had been unprofitable, and on June 1, 2000, the company adopted a plan to sell the assets of the division. The actual sale was effected on December 3, 2000, at a price of $1,200,000. The sale resulted in a before-tax gain of $300,000

The division incurred before-tax operating losses of $250,000 from the beginning of the year to May 31, and $60,000 from June 1 through December 3. The income tax rate is 40%. Chance's after-tax income from its continuing operations is $500,000.

Required:

Prepare an income statement for 2000 beginning with "income from continuing operations." Include appropriate EPS disclosures assuming 200,000 shares of common stock were outstanding throughout the year.

Exercise 3-3
Discontinued operations; disposal subsequent to year of measurement date

The Ottoboni Corporation had two operating divisions, one manufacturing division and a finance division. The finance division has been unprofitable, and on October 3, 2000, Ottoboni adopted a formal plan to sell the division. The sale was completed on March 19, 2001.

On October 3, 2000, the book value of the assets of the finance division was $2,100,000. The before-tax operating loss of the division from January 1, the beginning of the fiscal year, through October 2, 2000 was $200,000. The operating loss from October 3 through December 31 was $70,000. Also, the company estimated that the loss from operating the division from January 1, 2001 until the disposal date would approximate $120,000. The selling price of the division's assets was estimated to be $2,200,000. The company's effective tax rate is 40%. The after-tax income from continuing operations for 2000 is $600,000.

Required:

1. Prepare a partial income statement for 2000 beginning with income from continuing operations. Ignore EPS disclosures.
2. Repeat requirement 1 assuming that the estimated sales price of the finance division's assets was $2,600,000, instead of $2,200,000.

Exercise 3-4
Accounting change

The Rufus and Cleft Mining Company purchased machinery on June 15, 1998, for $2,500,000. A six-year life was estimated and a salvage value of $100,000 was anticipated. The company decided to use the straight-line depreciation method and recorded $600,000 in depreciation during 1998 and 1999. Early in 2000, the company revised the *total* estimated life of the machinery to 10 years. The estimated salvage value was revised to $200,000.

Required:

1. Briefly describe the accounting treatment for this change.
2. Determine depreciation for 2000.

Exercise 3-5
Statement of cash flows; classifications

The statement of cash flows classifies all cash inflows and outflows into one of the three categories shown below and lettered from a-c. In addition, certain transactions that do not involve cash are reported on the statement as noncash investing and financing activities, labeled d.

a) Operating activities
b) Investing activities
c) Financing activities
d) Noncash investing and financing activities

Required:

For each of the following transactions, use the letters above to indicate the appropriate classification category.

1. ____ Purchase of equipment in exchange for a note payable.
2. ____ Payment of rent.
3. ____ Collection of cash from customers.
4. ____ Payment of interest on debt.
5. ____ Purchase of a bond of another company.
6. ____ Issuance of common stock for cash.
7. ____ Sale of land for cash.
8. ____ Receipt of interest on a note receivable.
9. ____ Receipt of principal on a note receivable.
10. ____ Payment of cash dividends to shareholders.
11. ____ Payment to suppliers of inventory.

PROBLEMS

Problem 3-1
Comparative income statements; multiple-step format

Selected information about income statement accounts for the Ajax Company is presented below for the fiscal year ended December 31, 2000.

Sales	$6,200,000
Cost of goods sold	3,500,000
Administrative and selling expenses ..	1,500,000

Several events occurred during 2000 that have *not* yet been reflected in the above accounts:

1. A landslide caused $75,000 in uninsured damages to a warehouse. The landslide was considered to be an infrequent but not unusual event.
2. Interest revenue in the amount of $100,000 was earned.
3. The company sold some property in Alaska that it had been holding for 20 years. The sale resulted in a gain of $2 million. The company has no other investments in land and the transaction was considered to be both unusual and infrequent
4. The company incurred restructuring costs of $250,000
5. Interest expense on debt totaled $150,000.
6. Equipment was sold for a loss of $40,000.

Required:

Prepare a multiple-step income statement for the Ajax Company for the year 2000, including income taxes computed at 40%. Ignore EPS disclosures.

Problem 3-2
Discontinued operations; disposal subsequent to year of measurement date

The Tasmanian Candy Company reported income from continuing operations (after tax) of $1,000,000 for its fiscal year ended December 31, 2000. Tasmanian is discontinuing a major line of business. The plan to discontinue was adopted on August 6, 2000. The segment generated a before-tax operating loss of $90,000 for the period January 1 through August 6, 2000. The company anticipated a disposal date of April 1, 2001. The following are a number of situations, numbered 1 through 7, involving differing phase out period operating results, and gain/loss on disposal of the segment's assets.

Situation	Operating income (loss) from August 6 through December 31	Estimated operating income (loss) from January 1, 2001 through disposal	Estimated gain (loss) on sale of assets
1.	$360,000	$(240,000)	$300,000
2	(120,000)	(220,000)	(330,000)
3.	120,000	240,000	(500,000)
4.	500,000	(150,000)	300,000
5	400,000	150,000	300,000
6.	(120,000)	(70,000)	100,000
7.	(300,000)	(200,000)	650,000

Required:
For each of the situations, determine the appropriate gain (loss) on disposal of the segment that should be recognized in 2000 and 2001.

EXERCISES

Exercise 4-1
Construction accounting; percentage-of-completion and completed contract methods

The Ugenti Construction Company contracted to construct a warehouse building for $2,600,000. Construction began in 2000 and was completed in 2001. Data relating to the contract are summarized below:

	2000	2001
Costs incurred during the year	$ 360,000	$1,650,000
Estimated costs to complete as of 12/31 .	1,560,000	-
Billings during the year	430,000	2,130,000
Cash collections during the year.............	320,000	2,280,000

Required:

1. Compute the amount of gross profit or loss to be recognized in 2000 and 2001 using the percentage-of-completion method.
2. Compute the amount of gross profit or loss to be recognized in 2000 and 2001 using the completed contract method.
3. Prepare a partial balance sheet to show how the information related to this contract would be presented at the end of 2000 using the percentage-of completion method.
4. Prepare a partial balance sheet to show how the information related to this contract would be presented at the end of 2000 using the completed contract method.

Exercise 4-2
Percentage-of-completion method; loss projected on entire project

On April 13, 2000, the Pagano Construction Company entered into a three-year construction contract to build a mall for a price of $12,000,000. During 2000, costs of $3,000,000 were incurred with estimated costs of $6,000,000 yet to be incurred. Billings of $3,800,000 were sent and cash collected was $3,250,000.

In 2001, costs incurred were $4,000,000 with remaining costs estimated to be $5,600,000. 2001 billings were $3,500,000 and $3,600,000 cash was collected. The project was completed in 2002 after additional costs of $5,800,000 were incurred. The company's fiscal year-end is December 31. Arrow uses the percentage-of-completion method.

Required:

1. Calculate the amount of gross profit or loss to be recognized in each of the three years.
2. Prepare journal entries for 2000 and 2001 to record the transactions described (credit "Various accounts" for construction costs incurred).
3. Prepare a partial balance sheet to show the presentation of the project as of December 31, 2000 and 2001.

Exercise 4-3
Installment sales; alternative recognition methods

On June 1, 2000, the Luttman and Dowd Company sold inventory to the Ushman Corporation for $400,000. Terms of the sale called for a down payment of $100,000 and four annual installments of $75,000 due on each June 1, beginning June 1, 2001. Each installment also will include interest on the unpaid balance applying an appropriate interest rate. The inventory cost Foster $150,000. The company uses the perpetual inventory system.

Required:

1. Compute the amount of gross profit to be recognized from the installment sale in 2000, 2001, 2002, 2003, and 2004 using point of delivery revenue recognition. Ignore interest charges.
2. Repeat requirement 1 applying the installment sales method.
3. Repeat requirement 1 applying the cost recovery method.

Exercise 4-4
Franchise sales; revenue recognition

On November 15, 2000, the Coldstone Ice Cream Company entered into a franchise agreement with an individual. In exchange for an initial franchise fee of $25,000, Coldstone will provide initial services to the franchisee to include assistance in design and construction of the building, help in training employees, help in obtaining financing, and management advice over the first five years of the ten-year franchise agreement.

50% of the initial franchise fee is payable on November 15, 2000, with the remaining $12,500 payable in five equal annual installments beginning on November 15, 2001. These installments will include interest at an appropriate rate. The franchise opened for business on February 15, 2001.

Required:

Assume that the initial services to be performed by Coldstone subsequent to November 15, 2000, are substantial and that collectibility of the installment receivable is reasonably certain. Substantial performance of the initial services is deemed to have occurred when the franchise opened. Prepare the necessary journal entries for the following dates (ignoring interest charges):

1. November 15, 2000, and
2. February 15, 2001.

Exercise 4-5
Evaluating efficiency of asset management

The year 2000 income statement of Garret & Sons Music Company reported net sales of $10 million, cost of goods sold of $6 million, and net income of $1 million. The following table shows the company's comparative balance sheets for 2000 and 1999:

	($ in 000s)	
Assets:	**2000**	**1999**
Cash	$ 240	$ 280
Accounts receivable	800	600
Inventory	850	700
Property, plant, and equipment (net)	2,600	2,520
Total assets	$4,490	$4,100
Liabilities and Shareholders' Equity:		
Current liabilities	$ 720	$ 650
Notes payable	600	1,000
Paid-in capital	2,000	2,000
Retained earnings	1,170	450
Total liabilities and shareholders equity	$4,490	$4,100

Some industry averages for the company's line of business are:

inventory turnover	6	times
average collection period	28	days
asset turnover	2	times

Required:
Assess Garret & Son's asset management relative to its industry.

Exercise 4-6
Profitability ratios

The following condensed information was reported by Sanders Manufacturing, Inc. for 2000 and 1999:

	($ in 000s) 2000	1999
Income statement information:		
Net sales	$7,200	$6,800
Net income	360	408
Balance Sheet information:		
Current assets	$ 800	$ 750
Property, plant, and equipment (net)	2,100	1,950
Total assets	$2,900	$2,700
Current liabilities	$ 250	$ 400
Long-term liabilities	950	750
Paid-in capital	1,000	1,000
Retained earnings	700	550
Liabilities and shareholders' equity	$2,900	$2,700

Required:

1. Determine the following ratios for 2000:
   a. profit margin on sales
   b. return on assets
   c. return on shareholders' equity
2. Determine the amount of dividends paid to shareholders during 2000.

PROBLEMS

Problem 4-1
Percentage-of-completion method

In the year 2000, the Malinkrodt Construction Company entered into a contract to construct a road for Dade County for $15,000,000. The road was completed in 2002. Information related to the contract is as follows:

	2000	2001	2002
Costs incurred during the year	$4,000,000	$4,800,000	$4,200,000
Estimated costs to complete as of year-end	8,000,000	4,000,000	-
Billings during the year	3,500,000	5,000,000	6,500,000
Cash collections during the year..........	2,800,000	5,600,000	6,600,000

Malinkrodt uses the percentage-of-completion method of accounting for long-term construction contracts.

Required:

1. Calculate the amount of gross profit to be recognized in each of the three years.
2. Prepare all necessary journal entries for each of the years (credit "Various accounts" for construction costs incurred).
3. Prepare a partial balance sheet for 2000 and 2001 showing any items related to the contract.
4. Calculate the amount of gross profit to be recognized in each of the three years assuming the following costs incurred and costs to complete information:

	2000	2001	2002
Costs incurred during the year	$4,000,000	$4,200,000	$7,200,000
Estimated costs to complete as of year-end	8,000,000	7,100,000	-

Problem 4-2

Installment sales; alternative recognition methods

On October 31, 2000, the Dionne Company sold merchandise to the Parker Corporation for $800,000. Terms of the sale called for a down payment of $200,000 and three annual installments of $200,000 due on each October 31, beginning October 31, 2001. Each installment also will include interest on the unpaid balance applying an appropriate interest rate. The book value of the merchandise on Dionne's books on the date of sale was $400,000. The perpetual inventory system is used. The company's fiscal year end is December 31.

Required:

1. Prepare a table showing the amount of gross profit to be recognized in each of the four years of the installment sale applying each of the following methods:
   a. Point of delivery revenue recognition.
   b. Installment sales method.
   c. Cost recovery method.
2. Prepare journal entries for each of the four years applying the three revenue recognition methods listed in requirement 1. Ignore interest charges.
3. Prepare a partial balance sheet as of the end of 2000 and 2001 listing the items related to the installment sale applying each of the three methods listed in requirement 1.

EXERCISES

Exercise 5-1
Balance sheet classification

The following are the typical classifications used in a balance sheet:

a) Current assets
b) Investments and funds
c) Property, plant and equipment
d) Intangible assets
e) Other assets
f) Current liabilities
g) Long-term liabilities
h) Paid-in-capital
i) Retained earnings

Required:

For each of the following balance sheet items, use the letters above to indicate the appropriate classification category. If the item is a contra account (valuation account), place a minus sign before the chosen letter.

1. ____ Note receivable, due in 2 years
2. ____ Accounts receivable
3. ____ Accumulated depreciation
4. ____ Land, in use
5. ____ Note payable, due in 10 months
6. ____ Interest payable
7. ____ Note receivable, due in 6 months
8. ____ Cash equivalents
9. ____ Investment in ABC Corp., long-term
10. ____ Inventories
11. ____ Goodwill
12. ____ Accrued salaries payable
13 ____ Accrued interest payable
14 ____ Prepaid insurance
15. ____ Common stock
16. ____ Equipment
17. ____ Unearned revenue
18. ____ Warranties payable

Exercise 5-2
Balance sheet preparation

The following is a December 31, 2000, post-closing trial balance for the Curtis Corporation.

Account Title	Debits	Credits
Cash and cash equivalents	70,000	
Accounts receivable	110,000	
Inventories	120,000	
Prepaid insurance	3,000	
Investment in Qualcom stock, short-term	15,000	
Machinery and equipment	230,000	
Accumulated depreciation – machinery and equipment		111,000
Note receivable – long-term	50,000	
Interest receivable, due in 3 months	2,000	
Accounts payable		45,000
Wages payable		10,000
Interest payable		3,000
Bonds payable (due in ten years)		100,000
Common stock		200,000
Retained earnings		131,000
Totals	600,000	600,000

Required:

Prepare a classified balance sheet for Curtis Corporation at December 31, 2000.

Exercise 5-3
Financial disclosures

The following are typical disclosures that would appear in the notes accompanying financial statements. For each of the items listed, indicate where the disclosure would likely appear — either in (A) the significant accounting policies note, or (B) a separate note.

1. Depreciation method	A
2. Information on related party transactions	____
3. Method of accounting for acquisitions	____
4. Composition and details of long-term debt	____
5. Inventory method	____
6. Basis of revenue recognition	____
7. Major damage to a plant facility occurring after year-end	____
8. Composition of accrued liabilities	____

Exercise 5-4
Calculating ratios

The year 2000 balance sheet for the Tomassini Corporation is shown below.

Tomassini Corporation
Balance Sheet
December 31, 2000

Assets:	($ in 000s)
Cash	$ 150
Accounts receivable	400
Inventories	500
Property, plant, and equipment (net)	1,200
Total assets	$2,250
Liabilities and Shareholders' Equity:	
Current liabilities	$ 600
Long-term liabilities	500
Paid-in capital	1,000
Retained earnings	150
Total liabilities and shareholders' equity	$2,250

The company's 2000 income statement reported the following amounts ($ in thousands):

Net sales	$6,600
Interest expense	30
Income tax expense	200
Net income	260

Required:
Determine the following ratios for 2000:

a. current ratio
b. acid-test ratio
c. debt to equity ratio
d. times interest earned ratio

Exercise 5-5
Effect of management decisions on ratios

Most decisions made by management impact the ratios analysts use to evaluate performance. Indicate (by letter) whether each of the actions listed below will immediately increase (I), decrease (D), or have no effect (N) on the ratios shown. Assume each ratio is less than 1.0 before the action is taken.

Action	Current ratio	Acid-test ratio	Debt to equity ratio
1. Issuance of common stock for cash	____	____	____
2. Purchase of inventory on account	____	____	____
3. Receipt of cash from a customer on account	____	____	____
4. Expiration of prepaid rent	____	____	____
5. Payment of a cash dividend	____	____	____
6. Purchase of equipment with a 6-month note	____	____	____
7. Purchase of long-term investment for cash	____	____	____
8. Sale of equipment for cash (no gain or loss)	____	____	____
9. Write-off of obsolete inventory	____	____	____
10. Decision to refinance on a long-term basis currently-maturing debt	____	____	____

PROBLEMS

Problem 5-1
Balance sheet preparation

The following is a December 31, 2000, post-closing trial balance for the Alexandria Exploration Corporation.

Account Title	Debits	Credits
Cash	52,000	
Accounts receivable	223,000	
Allowance for uncollectible accounts		15,000
Inventories	200,000	
Supplies	3,000	
Investments	140,000	
Land	100,000	
Buildings	500,000	
Accumulated depreciation - buildings		150,000
Machinery	250,000	
Accumulated depreciation - machinery		80,000
Goodwill (net of amortization)	36,000	
Accounts payable		125,000
Bonds payable		500,000
Interest payable		40,000
Common stock		500,000
Retained earnings		94,000
Totals	1,504,000	1,504,000

Additional information:

1. Accounts receivable includes a $50,000 note receivable received from a customer that is due in 2002. Also included is interest on the note of $3,000 that is due in six months.
2. The land account includes land that cost $20,000 that the company has not used and is currently listed for sale.
3. The investment account includes a $10,000, 3-month certificate of deposit due in 40 days. The remaining investments will be sold within the next year.
4. The bonds payable account consists of the following:
   a. a $200,000 issue due in six months.
   b. a $300,000 issue due in six years.
5. The common stock account represents 500,000 shares of no par value common stock issued and outstanding. The corporation has 1,000,000 shares authorized.

Required:
Prepare a classified balance sheet for Alexandria at December 31, 2000.

Problem 5-2
Balance sheet preparation

Presented below is the balance sheet for the Tillamoo Cheese Company at December 31, 2000.

Current assets	$ 740,000	Current liabilities	$ 620,000
Investments	300,000	Long-term liabilities	1,000,000
Property, plant and equipment	2,450,000	Shareholders' equity	2,170,000
Intangible assets	300,000		
Total assets	$3,790,000	Total liabilities and shareholders' equity ..	$3,790,000

The captions shown in the summarized statement above include the following:

a. Current assets: cash, $170,000; cash equivalents, $20,000; accounts receivable, $300,000; inventories, $235,000; and prepaid expenses, $15,000.
b. Investments: investments in common stock, short-term, $40,000; investments in bonds of other corporations, long-term, $260,000.
c. Property, plant, and equipment: buildings, $1,200,000 less accumulated depreciation, $300,000; equipment, $900,000 less accumulated depreciation, $300,000; and land, $950,000.
d. Intangible assets: patent, $80,000; and goodwill, $220,000.
e. Current liabilities: accounts payable, $260,000; notes payable, short-term, $180,000, and long-term, $100,000; interest payable, $20,000; and other accrued liabilities, $60,000
f. Long-term liabilities: bonds payable due 2006.
g. Shareholders' equity: common stock, $1,500,000; retained earnings, $670,000.

Required:

Prepare a corrected classified balance sheet for Tillamoo at December 31, 2000.

EXERCISES

Exercise 6-1
Future value; single amount

Determine the future value of the following single amounts:

	Invested Amount	Interest Rate	No. of Periods
1.	$50,000	8%	10
2.	30,000	6	20
3.	40,000	10	30
4.	60,000	4	12

Exercise 6-2
Present value; single amount

Determine the present value of the following single amounts:

	Future Amount	Interest Rate	No. of Periods
1.	$20,000	8%	10
2.	10,000	6	20
3.	25,000	10	30
4.	40,000	12	8

Exercise 6-3
Present value; annuities

Using the appropriate present value table and assuming a 10% annual interest rate, determine the present value on December 31, 2000, of a five-period annual annuity of $10,000 under each of the following situations:

1. The first payment is received on December 31, 2001, and interest is compounded annually.
2. The first payment is received on December 31, 2000, and interest is compounded annually.

Exercise 6-4
Solving for unknowns; single amounts

For each of the following situations involving single amounts, solve for the unknown (?). Assume that interest is compounded annually. (i = interest rate, and n = number of years)

	Present Value	Future Value	i	n
1.	?	$50,000	8%	10
2.	$31,947	70,000	?	20
3.	9,576	40,000	10	?
4.	20,462	100,000	?	14
5.	15,000	?	6	30

Exercise 6-5
Solving for unknowns; annuities

For each of the following situations involving annuities, solve for the unknown (?). Assume that interest is compounded annually and that all annuity amounts are received at the *end* of each period. (*i* = interest rate, and *n* = number of years)

	Present Value	Annuity Amount	i	n
1.	?	$ 5,000	10%	10
2.	$298,058	60,000	?	8
3.	337,733	30,000	8	?
4.	600,000	74,435	?	15
5.	200,000	?	12	6

Exercise 6-6
Deferred annuities; solving for annuity amount

On June 1, 2000, April Smith purchased carpeting from the Wearwell Carpet Company for $4,800. In order to increase sales, Wearwell allows customers to pay in installments and will defer any payments for 12 months. April will make 18 equal monthly payments, beginning June 1, 2001. The annual interest rate implicit in this agreement is 24%.

Required:

Calculate the monthly payment necessary for April to pay for her purchases.

PROBLEMS

Problem 6-1
Present and Future Value

The Reuter Company is facing several decisions regarding investing and financing activities. Address each decision independently.

1. On May 31, 2000, Reuter purchased equipment and agreed to pay the vendor $50,000 on the purchase date and the balance in four annual installments of $20,000 on each May 31 beginning May 31, 2001. Assuming that an interest rate of 8% properly reflects the time value of money in this situation, at what amount should Reuter value the equipment?
2. Reuter needs to accumulate sufficient funds to pay a $600,000 debt that comes due on December 31, 2004. The company will accumulate the funds by making four equal annual deposits to an account paying 4% interest compounded annually. Determine the required annual deposit if the first deposit is made on December 31, 2001.
3. Reuter needs to decide whether to lease or buy an office building. The purchase price of the building would be $2,000,000. If the lease option is chosen, the lease agreement would require 20 annual payments of $200,000 beginning immediately. A 10% interest rate is implicit in the lease agreement. Which option, buy or lease, should Reuter choose? Assume zero residual value if the buy option is chosen.

Problem 6-2
Deferred annuities

Smokey Sims is 60 years old and has been asked to accept early retirement from his company. The company has offered three alternative compensation packages to induce Smokey to retire:

1. $400,000 cash payment to be paid immediately.
2. A 15-year annuity of $40,000 beginning immediately.
3. A 15-year annuity of $45,000 beginning at age 65.

Required:

Which alternative should Smokey choose assuming that he is able to invest funds at a 6% rate?

Section 2

Economic Resources

EXERCISES

Exercise 7-1
Bank reconciliation and adjusting entries

The Harrison Company maintains a checking account at the Bank of Milwaukee. The bank provides a bank statement along with canceled checks on the last day of each month. The August, 2000 bank statement included the following information:

Balance, August 1, 2000	$ 68,326
Deposits	245,300
Checks processed	(236,222)
Service charges	(50)
NSF checks	(680)
Monthly deposit into savings account deducted directly by bank from account	(2,000)
Balance, August 31, 2000	$ 74,674

The company's general ledger account had a balance of $78,984 at the end of August. Deposits outstanding totaled $8,200 and all checks written by the company were processed by the bank except for those totaling $8,420. In addition, a $2,000 check to a supplier correctly recorded by the bank was incorrectly recorded by the company as a $200 credit to cash.

Required:
1. Prepare a bank reconciliation for the month of August.
2. Prepare the necessary journal entries at the end of August to adjust the general ledger cash account.

Exercise 7-2
Trade and cash discounts; the gross method and the net method compared

CCM Corporation, a manufacturer of furnaces, sold 200 units to a customer on April 6, 2000. The units have a list price of $800 each, but the customer was given a 20% trade discount. The terms of the sale were 1/10, n30.

Required:
1. Prepare the journal entries to record the sale on April 6 (ignore cost of goods) and payment on April 16, 2000, assuming that the gross method of accounting for cash discounts is used.
2. Prepare the journal entries to record the sale on April 6 (ignore cost of goods) and payment on May 6, 2000, assuming that the gross method of accounting for cash discounts is used.
3. Repeat requirements 1. and 2. assuming that the *net* method of accounting for cash discounts is used.

Exercise 7-3
Uncollectible accounts; allowance method; balance sheet approach

The Gadzooks Chip Company offers credit terms to its customers. At the end of 2000, accounts receivable totaled $2,223,000. The allowance method is used to account for uncollectible accounts. The allowance for uncollectible accounts had a credit balance of $68,000 at the beginning of 2000 and $46,200 in receivables were written off during the year as uncollectible. No previously written off receivables were collected. The company estimates bad debts by applying a percentage of 3% to accounts receivable at the end of the year.

Required:

1. Prepare journal entries to record the write-off of receivables and the year-end adjusting entry for bad debt expense.
2. How would accounts receivable be shown in the 2000 year-end balance sheet?

Exercise 7-4
Noninterest-bearing note receivable

On March 31, 2000, the Applix Corporation sold some merchandise to a customer for $80,000 and agreed to accept as payment a noninterest-bearing note with a 6% discount rate requiring the payment of $80,000 on March 31, 2001.

Required:

1. Prepare journal entries to record the sale of merchandise (omit any entry that might be required for the cost of the goods sold), the December 31, 2000 interest accrual, and the March 31 collection.
2. What is the *effective* interest rate on the note?

Exercise 7-5
Factoring of accounts receivable without recourse

The Fullbright Book Company transferred $100,000 of accounts receivable to the American Trust Bank. The transfer was made *without recourse*. American Trust assesses a finance charge equal to 1% of accounts receivable transferred. The bank will collect the receivables directly from Fullbright's customers.

Required:

Prepare the journal entry to record the transfer on the books of Fullbright.

Exercise 7-6
Factoring of accounts receivable with recourse

[This is a variation of the previous exercise modified to focus on factoring with recourse.]

The Fullbright Book Company transferred $100,000 of accounts receivable to the American Trust Bank. The transfer was made *with recourse*. American Trust assesses a finance charge equal to 1% of accounts receivable transferred. The bank will collect the receivables directly from Fullbright's customers.

Required:

1. Prepare the journal entry to record the transfer on the books of Fullbright assuming that the "sale" criteria are met.
2. Repeat requirement 1 assuming that the "sale" criteria are *not* met.

Exercise 7-7
Discounting a note receivable

The Falletti Pasta Company obtained a $50,000 note receivable from a customer on June 1, 2000. The note, along with interest at 8%, is due on June 1, 2001. On September 1, 2000, Falletti discounted the note at the Bank of Los Alimos. The bank's discount rate is 10%.

Required:

1. Prepare the journal entries required on September 1, 2000, to accrue interest and to record the discounting (round all calculations to the nearest dollar) for Falletti. Assume that the discounting is accounted for as a sale.
2. Record the discounting assuming that it is accounted for as a loan.

PROBLEMS

Problem 7-1
Uncollectible accounts; allowance method; income statement and balance sheet approach

SDLI, Inc. grants its customers 30 days credit. The company uses the allowance method for its uncollectible accounts receivable. During the year, a monthly bad debt accrual is made by multiplying 2% times the amount of credit sales for the month. At the fiscal year-end of December 31, an aging of accounts receivable schedule is prepared and the allowance for uncollectible accounts is adjusted accordingly.

At the end of 1999, accounts receivable were $1,250,000 and the allowance account had a credit balance of $106,000. Accounts receivable activity for 2000 was as follows:

Beginning balance	$1,250,000
Credit sales	3,800,000
Collections	(3,745,000)
Write-offs	(82,000)
Ending balance	$1,223,000

The company's controller prepared the following aging summary of year-end accounts receivable:

Summary

Age Group	Amount	Percent Uncollectible
0-60 days	$ 825,000	2%
61-90 days	220,000	10%
91-120 days	50,000	30%
Over 120 days	128,000	40%
Total	$1,223,000	

Required:

1. Prepare a summary journal entry to record the monthly bad debt accrual and the write-offs during the year.
2. Prepare the necessary year-end adjusting entry for bad debt expense.
3. What is total bad debt expense for 2000? How would accounts receivable appear in the 2000 balance sheet?

Problem 7-2
Miscellaneous receivable transactions

The Appomatix Company sells fertilizer and pesticides to wholesalers. The company's fiscal year-end is December 31. During 2000, the following transactions related to receivables occurred:

March 31	Sold merchandise to the Misthos Co. and accepted a noninterest-bearing note with a discount rate of 10%. The $12,000 payment is due on March 31, 2001.
April 12	Sold merchandise to Able Co. for $10,000 with terms 2/10, n30. Appomatix uses the gross method to account for cash discounts.
April 21	Collected the entire amount due from Able Co.
April 27	A customer returned merchandise costing Apppomatix $6,000. Appomatix reduced the customers receivable balance by $8,000, the sales price of the merchandise. Sales returns are recorded by the company as they occur.
May 30	Transferred receivables of $100,000 to a factor without recourse. The factor charged Appomatix a 2% finance charge on the receivables transferred.
July 31	Sold merchandise to Favre Corporation for $15,000 and accepted an 8%, 6-month note. 8% is an appropriate rate for this type of note.
Sept. 30	Discounted the Favre Corporation note at the bank. The bank's discount rate is 12%. The note was discounted without recourse.

Required:

1. Prepare the necessary journal entries for Appomatix for each of the above dates. For transactions involving the sale of merchandise, ignore the entry for the cost of goods sold (Round all calculations to the nearest dollar).
2. Prepare any necessary adjusting entries at December 31, 2000. Adjusting entries are only recorded at year-end (Round all calculations to the nearest dollar).

EXERCISES

Exercise 8-1
Perpetual and periodic inventory systems compared

The following information is available for the Kleinschmidt Corporation for 2000:

Beginning inventory	$112,000
Merchandise purchases (on account)	265,000
Freight charges on purchases (on account)	16,000
Merchandise returned to supplier (for credit)	6,000
Ending inventory	123,000
Sales (on account)	350,000
Cost of merchandise sold	264,000

Required:

Applying both a perpetual and a periodic inventory system, prepare the journal entries that summarize the transactions that created these balances. Include all end-of-period adjusting entries indicated.

Exercise 8-2
Trade and purchase discounts; the gross method and the net method compared

The Kavendish Company, a manufacturer of commercial-use washing machines, sold 50 units to the E-z Sleep Motel chain on January 14, 2000. The units have a list price of $800 each, but E-z Sleep was given a 25% trade discount. The terms of the sale were 2/10, n30. E-z Sleep uses a periodic inventory system.

Required:

1. Prepare the journal entries to record the purchase by E-z Sleep on January 14 and payment on January 23, 2000, using the gross method of accounting for purchase discounts.
2. Prepare the journal entries to record the purchase on January 14 and payment on February 13, 2000, using the gross method of accounting for purchase discounts.
3. Repeat requirements 1 and 2 using the *net* method of accounting for purchase discounts.

Exercise 8-3
Goods in transit; consignment

The December 31, 2000, year-end inventory balance of the Delphi Printing Company is $317,000. You have been asked to review the following transactions to determine if they have been correctly recorded.

1. Materials purchased from a supplier and shipped to Delphi f.o.b. destination on December 28, 2000, were received on January 2, 2001. The invoice cost of $50,000 is *not* included in the preliminary inventory balance.
2. At year-end, Delphi had $12,000 of merchandise on consignment from the Harvey Company. This merchandise *is* included in the preliminary inventory balance.
3. On December 29, merchandise costing $17,000 was shipped to a customer f.o.b. shipping point and arrived at the customer's location on January 3, 2001. The merchandise is *not* included in the preliminary inventory balance.
4. Materials purchased from a supplier and shipped to Delphi f.o.b. shipping point on December 28, 2000 were received on January 4, 2001. The invoice cost of $32,000 is *not* included in the preliminary inventory balance.

Required:
Determine the correct inventory amount to be reported on Delphi's 2000 balance sheet.

Exercise 8-4
Inventory cost flow methods; perpetual system

The Alpensose Milk Company uses a *perpetual* inventory system. The following transactions affected its merchandise inventory during the month of March, 2000:

March 1 — Inventory on hand — 3,000 units; cost $8.00 each.
March 8 — Purchased 5,000 units for $8.40 each.
March 14 — Sold 4,000 units for $14.00 each.
March 18 — Purchased 6,000 units for $8.20 each.
March 25 — Sold 7,000 units for $14.00 each.
March 31 — Inventory on hand — 3,000 units.

Required:
Determine the inventory balance Alpensose would report on its March 31, 2000, balance sheet and the cost of goods sold it would report on its March, 2000, income statement using each of the following cost flow methods:

1. First-in, first-out (FIFO)
2. Last-in, first-out (LIFO)
3. Average cost

Exercise 8-5
Average cost method; periodic and perpetual systems

The following information is taken from the inventory records of the Bauxite Company:

Beginning inventory, 4/1/00	7,000 units @ $22.00
Purchases:	
4/5	6,000 units @ $22.65
4/26	9,000 units @ $24.00
Sales:	
4/11	5,000 units
4/28	8,000 units

9,000 units were on hand at the end of April.

Required:

1. Assuming that Bauxite uses a periodic inventory system and employs the average cost method, determine cost of goods sold for September and September's ending inventory.
2. Repeat requirement 1 assuming that the company uses a perpetual inventory system.

Exercise 8-6
Dollar-value LIFO

On January 1, 2000, the Delbridge Company adopted the dollar-value LIFO method for its one inventory pool. The pool's value on this date was $832,000. The 2000 and 2001 ending inventory valued at year-end costs were $954,000 and $975,000, respectively. The appropriate cost indexes are 1.02 for 2000 and 1.05 for 2001.

Required:

Calculate the inventory value at the end of 2000 and 2001 using the dollar-value LIFO method.

PROBLEMS

Problem 8-1
Various inventory transactions; determining inventory and cost of goods sold

The Helmut and King Corporation began 2000 with inventory of 8,000 units of its only product. The units cost $10.00 each. The company uses a periodic inventory system and the LIFO cost method. The following transactions occurred during 2000:

1. Purchased 40,000 additional units at a cost of $11.00 per unit. Terms of the purchases were 2/10, n30, and 80% of the purchases were paid for within the 10 day discount period. The company uses the gross method to record purchase discounts. The merchandise was purchased f.o.b. shipping point and freight charges of $1.00 per unit were paid by Helmut and King.
2. Sales for the year totaled 46,000 units at $20.00 per unit.
3. On December 28, 2000, Helmut and King purchased 5,000 additional units at $12.00 each (price includes freight of $1.00 per unit). The goods were shipped f.o.b. shipping point and arrived at Helmut and King's warehouse on January 4, 2001. The terms of the purchase were n30.
4. 2,000 units were on hand at the end of 2000.

Required:
Determine ending inventory and cost of goods sold for 2000.

Problem 8-2
Various inventory costing methods

Callahan & Sons began 2000 with 10,000 units of its principle product. The cost of each unit is $25.00. Merchandise transactions for the month of January, 2000, are as follows:

Purchases

Date of Purchase	Units	Unit Cost*	Total Cost
Jan. 4	8,000	$ 24.00	$192,000
Jan. 22	7,000	27.00	189,000
Totals	15,000		$381,000

* includes purchase price and cost of freight.

Sales for the month totaled 13,000 units, leaving 12,000 units on hand at the end of the month.

Required:
Calculate January's ending inventory and cost of goods sold for the month using each of the following alternatives:

1. FIFO, periodic system
2. LIFO, periodic system
3. Average cost, periodic system

EXERCISES

Exercise 9-1
Lower-of-cost-or-market

Cooperstown Sports, Inc. has four products in its inventory. Information about the December 31, 2000, inventory is as follows:

Product	Total Cost	Total Replacement Cost	Total Net Realizable Value
Gloves	$360,000	$330,000	$300,000
Bats	260,000	240,000	320,000
Balls	150,000	110,000	125,000
Uniforms	600,000	560,000	950,000

The normal gross profit percentage is 20 percent of *cost*.

Required:

1. Determine the balance sheet inventory carrying value at December 31, 2000, assuming the LCM rule is applied to individual products.
2. Assuming that Cooperstown recognizes an inventory write-down as a separate income statement item, determine the amount of the loss.

Exercise 9-2
Gross profit method

A fire destroyed a warehouse of the Nicklaus Tire Company on June 17, 2000. Accounting records on that date indicated the following:

Merchandise inventory, January 1, 2000	$ 4,500,000
Purchases to date	14,500,000
Freight-in	1,000,000
Sales to date	23,000,000

The gross profit ratio has averaged 40% of sales for the past three years.

Required:

Use the gross profit method to estimate the cost of the inventory destroyed in the fire.

Exercise 9-3
Retail inventory method; average cost

The Alcala Clothing Goods Store uses a periodic inventory system and the retail inventory method to estimate ending inventory and cost of goods sold. The following data is available for the month of May, 2000:

	Cost	Retail
Beginning inventory	$ 40,000	$60,000
Net purchases	28,250	37,000
Net markups		2,000
Net markdowns		1,500
Net sales		45,000

Required:

Estimate the average cost of ending inventory and cost of goods sold for May. Do not approximate LCM.

Exercise 9-4
Conventional retail method; normal spoilage

The Goodwin Department Store uses the retail inventory method to estimate ending inventory and cost of goods sold. Data for the year 2000 is as follows:

	Cost	Retail
Beginning inventory	$ 180,000	$ 300,000
Purchases	1,479,000	2,430,000
Freight in	30,000	
Purchase returns	60,000	105,000
Net markups		90,000
Net markdowns		45,000
Normal spoilage		63,000
Net sales		2,340,000

Required:
Estimate the ending inventory and cost of goods sold for 2000, applying the conventional retail method (average, LCM).

Exercise 9-5
Dollar-value LIFO retail

On January 1, 2000, the Goldenrod Glass Company adopted the dollar-value LIFO retail method. The following data is available for the year 2000:

	Cost	Retail
Beginning inventory	$213,840	$396,000
Net purchases	360,000	765,000
Net markups		18,000
Net markdowns		33,000
Net sales		690,000
Retail price index, 12/31/00		1.02

Required:
Calculate the estimated ending inventory and cost of goods sold for 2000.

Exercise 9-6
Inventory error

In the year 2000, the internal auditors of Abbott Research, Inc. discovered that goods costing $1.6 million that were shipped f.o.b. shipping point in December of 1999 were in transit on 12/31/99. The goods were recorded as a purchase in December of 1999 but were not included in the 1999 year-end inventory.

Required:
Prepare the journal entry needed in 2000 to correct the error. Also, briefly describe any other measures Abbott Research would take in connection with correcting the error. (Ignore income taxes.)

PROBLEMS

Problem 9-1
Retail inventory method; various cost methods

Infomania Corporation uses the retail inventory method to estimate ending inventory and cost of goods sold. Data for the year 2000 is as follows:

	Cost	Retail
Beginning inventory	$140,000	$280,000
Purchases	420,000	690,000
Freight in	16,000	
Purchase returns	12,000	18,000
Net markups		24,000
Net markdowns		26,000
Normal spoilage		5,000
Abnormal spoilage		10,000
Sales		700,000
Sales returns		20,000
Employee discounts		6,000

The company records sales net of employee discounts.

Required:
Estimate Infomania's ending inventory and cost of goods sold for the year using the retail inventory method and the following applications:

1. Average cost.
2. Conventional (average, LCM)

Problem 9-2
Dollar-value LIFO retail method

The Adirondock Company maintains inventory records at selling prices as well as at cost. For the year 2000, the records indicate the following data:

($ in 000s)	Cost	Retail
Beginning inventory	$ 128	$ 200
Purchases	1,072	1,600
Freight-in on purchases	59	
Purchase returns	2	3
Net markups		6
Net markdowns		13
Net sales		1,465

Required:
Assuming the price level increased from 1.00 at January 1 to 1.08 at December 31, 2000, use the dollar-value LIFO retail method to approximate cost of ending inventory and cost of goods sold.

EXERCISES

Exercise 10-1
Goodwill

The Hermanson and Jones Corporation purchased all of the outstanding common stock of Viacon Corporation for $25,000,000 in cash. The book value of Viacon's net assets (assets minus liabilities) was $16,250,000. The fair values of all of Viacon's assets and liabilities were equal to their book values with the following exceptions:

	Book Value	**Fair Value**
Receivables	$3,000,000	$2,850,000
Property, plant, and equipment	10,200,000	11,200,000
Intangible assets	30,000	3,000,000

Required:
Calculate the amount paid for goodwill.

Exercise 10-2
Acquisition cost; noninterest-bearing note

On January 1, 2000, the Farmington Corporation purchased a packaging and labeling machine. Farmington paid $25,000 down and signed a noninterest-bearing note requiring six annual installments of $10,000 to be paid on each December 31 beginning December 31, 2000. The fair value of the machine is not determinable. An interest rate of 8% properly reflects the time value of money in this situation.

Required:
1. Prepare the journal entry to record the acquisition of the machine. Round computations to the nearest dollar.
2. Prepare the journal entry to record the first payment on December 31, 2000. Round computations to the nearest dollar.
3. Prepare the journal entry to record the second payment on December 31, 2001. Round computations to the nearest dollar.

Exercise 10-3
Nonmonetary exchange; similar assets

The Pioline Company recently traded in a pick-up truck for a newer model truck. The old truck's book value was $1,000 (original cost of $13,000 less $12,000 in accumulated depreciation) and its fair value was $800. Pioline paid $14,000 to complete the exchange.

Required:
Prepare the journal entry to record the exchange.

Exercise 10-4
Nonmonetary exchange; similar assets

[This is a variation of the previous exercise.]

Required:
Assume the same facts as in Exercise 10-3, except that the fair value of the old truck is $1,500. Prepare the journal entry to record the exchange.

Exercise 10-5
Research and development

The Best and Krieg Company incurred the following research and development costs during 2000:

Salaries and wages for lab research	$ 350,000
Materials used in R&D projects	400,000
Purchase of equipment	85,000
Fees paid to outsiders for R&D projects performed by the outsiders for Best and Krieg	465,000
Patent filing and legal costs for a developed product	20,000
In-process research and development (related to the acquisition of Radon, Inc.)	1,200,000
Total	$2,520,000

The equipment has a 3-year life and has no value beyond the current research project for which it was acquired.

Required:
Calculate the amount of research and development expense that Best and Krieg should report in its 2000 income statement.

Exercise 10-6
Software development costs

Early in the year 2000, the Adonis Software Company began developing a new software package to be marketed. The project was completed in December of 2000 at a cost of $10 million. Of this amount, $6 million was spent before technological feasibility was established. Adonis expects a useful life of three years for the new product with total revenues of $20 million. During 2001, revenue of $5 million was recognized.

Required:
1. Prepare a journal entry to record the 2000 development costs.
2. Calculate the required amortization for 2001.
3. At what amount should the computer software costs be reported in the December 31, 2001 balance sheet?

PROBLEMS

Problem 10-1
Nonmonetary exchange

On October 15, 2000, the Brown Company exchanged operational assets with the Filzinger Corporation. The facts of the exchange are as follows:

	Brown's Asset	Filzinger's Asset
Original cost	$300,000	$278,000
Accumulated depreciation	200,000	220,000
Fair market value	125,000	85,000

To equalize the exchange, Filzinger paid Brown $40,000 in cash.

Required:

1. Assuming that the assets exchanged are considered *dissimilar* for both companies, record the exchange for both Brown and Filzinger.
2. Assuming that the assets exchanged are considered *similar* for both companies, record the exchange for both Brown and Filzinger.

Problem 10-2
Interest capitalization; specific interest method

On January 1, 2000, the Edinger Manufacturing Company began construction of a building to be used as its office headquarters. The building was completed on June 30, 2001.

Expenditures on the project were as follows:

January 3, 2000	$500,000
March 31, 2000	600,000
June 30, 2000	800,000
October 31, 2000	600,000
January 31, 2001	300,000
March 31, 2001	500,000
May 31, 2001	600,000

On January 3, 2000, the company obtained a $2 million construction loan with a 10% interest rate. The loan was outstanding all of 2000 and 2001. The company's other interest-bearing debt included a long-term note of $5,000,000 with an 8% interest rate, and a mortgage of $3,000,000 on another building with an interest rate of 6%. Both debts were outstanding during all of 2000 and 2001. The company's fiscal year end is December 31.

Required:

1. Calculate the amount of interest that Edinger should capitalize in 2000 and 2001 using the *specific interest method.*
2. What is the total cost of the building?
3. Calculate the amount of interest expense that will appear in the 2000 and 2001 income statements.

EXERCISES

Exercise 11-1
Depreciation methods

On January 1, 2000, the Pattison Corporation purchased machinery for $240,000. The estimated useful life of the machinery is eight years and the estimated residual value is $20,000. The machine is expected to produce 55,000 units during its useful life.

Required:

Calculate depreciation for 2000 and 2001 using each of the following methods. Round all computations to the nearest dollar.

1. Straight-line.
2. Sum-of-the-years' digits.
3. Double-declining balance.
4. One hundred fifty percent declining balance.
5. Units-of-production (units produced in 2000, 8,000; units produced in 2001, 12,000).

Exercise 11-2
Depreciation methods; partial years

[This is a variation of the previous exercise modified to focus on depreciation for partial years.]

On April 30, 2000, the Pattison Corporation purchased machinery for $240,000. The estimated useful life of the machinery is eight years and the estimated residual value is $20,000. The machine is expected to produce 55,000 units during its useful life.

Required:

Calculate depreciation for 2000 and 2001 using each of the following methods. Partial year depreciation is calculated based on the number of months the asset is in service. Round all computations to the nearest dollar.

1. Straight-line.
2. Sum-of-the-years' digits.
3. Double-declining balance.
4. One hundred fifty percent declining balance.
5. Units-of-production (units produced in 2000, 6,000; units produced in 2001, 12,000).

Exercise 11-3
Depletion

On March 31, 2000, the Allegheny Mining Company purchased the rights to a coal mine. The purchase price plus additional costs necessary to prepare the mine for extraction of the coal totaled $2,000,000. The company expects to extract 1,000,000 tons of coal during a three-year period. During 2000, 400,000 tons were extracted and sold immediately.

Required:

1. Calculate depletion for 2000.
2. Discuss the accounting treatment of the depletion calculated in requirement 1.

Exercise 11-4
Amortization

The Leidecker Company provided the following information on intangible assets:

a. A patent was purchased for $1,000,000 on June 30, 1998. Leidecker estimated the remaining useful life of the patent to be five years.
b. During 2000, a franchise was purchased from the Taco Tio Company for $40,000. The contractual life of the franchise is 20 years and Leidecker records a full year of amortization in the year of purchase.
c. Effective January 1, 2000, based on new events that have occurred, Leidecker estimates that the remaining life of the patent is seven more years.

Required:
1. Prepare the entries necessary to reflect the above information for 1998 through 2000, including year-end adjusting entries to record amortization.
2. Prepare a schedule showing the intangible asset section of the company's December 31, 2000, balance sheet.

Exercise 11-5
Change in estimate; useful life and residual value of equipment

Evergreen Ltd. purchased a cold storage unit on January 2, 1997, at a cost of $640,000. The unit was depreciated using the straight-line method over an estimated 10-year useful life with an estimated residual value of $40,000. On January 1, 2000, the estimate of useful life was changed to a total of 12 years, and the estimate of residual value was changed to $20,000.

Required:
Prepare the appropriate adjusting entry for depreciation in 2000 to reflect the revised estimate.

Exercise 11-6
Error correction

In 2000, the assistant controller of Paddington Industries discovered that in 1997 the company had debited research and development expense for the $200,000 cost of a machine purchased on January 3, 1997. The machine was purchased with the intention that it be used on many different research projects over an expected useful life of eight years. Straight-line depreciation is used by Paddington and residual value is always set at 10% of cost.

Required:
Prepare the appropriate correcting entry assuming the error was **discovered in 2000** before the adjusting and closing entries. (Ignore income taxes.)

PROBLEMS

Problem 11-1
Partial year depreciation; asset addition; increase in useful life

On May 1, 1998, the Sanderson Electrical Company purchased equipment to be used in its manufacturing process. The equipment cost $60,000, has a six-year useful life and no residual value. The company uses the straight-line depreciation method for all manufacturing equipment.

On January 4, 2000, $15,000 was spent to repair the equipment and to add a feature that increased its operating efficiency. Of the total expenditure, $4,000 represented ordinary repairs and annual maintenance and $11,000 represented the cost of the new feature. In addition to increasing operating efficiency, the total useful life of the equipment was extended to eight years.

Required:

Prepare journal entries for the following:

1. Depreciation for 1998 and 1999.
2. The 2000 expenditure.
3. Depreciation for 2000.

Problem 11-2
Straight-line depreciation; change in useful life and residual value

The property, plant and equipment section of the Winderl Company's December 31, 1999, balance sheet contained the following:

Property, plant, and equipment:		
Land		$410,000
Building	$1,250,000	
Less: accumulated depreciation	300,000	950,000
Equipment	$540,000	
Less: accumulated depreciation	?	?
Total property, plant and equipment		?

The land and building were purchased at the beginning of 1995. Straight-line depreciation is used and a residual value of $50,000 for the building is anticipated. The equipment is comprised of the following three machines:

Machine	**Cost**	**Date Acquired**	**Residual Value**	**Life in years**
651	$150,000	1/1/97	$10,000	10
652	280,000	6/30/97	- 0 -	7
653	110,000	10/1/99	5,000	8

Early in 2000, the useful life of machine 651 was revised to eight years in total, and the residual value was revised to zero.

Required:

1. Calculate the accumulated depreciation on the equipment at December 31, 1999.
2. Prepare the 2000 year-end adjusting journal entries to record depreciation on the building and equipment.

Section 3

Financial Instruments

EXERCISES

Exercise 12-1
Various transactions related to securities available for sale

Parnell Industries buys securities to be available for sale when circumstances warrant, *not* to profit from short-term differences in price and *not* necessarily to hold debt securities to maturity. The following selected transactions relate to investment activities of Parnell Industries whose fiscal year ends on December 31. No investments were held by Parnell at the beginning of the year.

2000

March 1	Purchased 2 million Platinum Gems, Inc. common shares for $124 million, including brokerage fees and commissions.
April 13	Purchased $200 million of 10% bonds at face value from Oracle Wholesale Corporation.
July 20	Received cash dividends of $3 million on the investment in Platinum Gems, Inc. common shares.
October 13	Received semiannual interest of $10 million on the investment in Oracle bonds.
October 14	Sold the Oracle bonds for $205 million.
November 1	Purchased 500,000 SPI International preferred shares for $40 million, including brokerage fees and commissions.
December 31	Recorded the necessary adjusting entry(s) relating to the investments. The market prices of the investments are $64 per share for Platinum Gems, Inc. and $74 per share for SPI International preferred shares.

2001

January 25	Sold half the Platinum Gems, Inc. shares for $65 per share.
March 1	Sold the SPI International preferred shares for $78 per share.

Required:

1. Prepare the appropriate journal entry for each transaction or event.
2. Show the amounts that would be reported on the company's 2000 income statement relative to these investments.

Exercise 12-2
Various investment securities

At December 31, 2000, McKnight Brothers Corp. had the following investments that were purchased during 2000, its first year of operations:

		Cost	*Fair Value*
Trading Securities:			
Security	A	$ 700,000	$ 725,000
	B	210,000	200,000
Totals		$ 910,000	$ 925,000
Securities Available for Sale:			
Security	C	$ 500,000	$ 560,000
	D	850,000	865,000
Totals		$1,350,000	$1,425,000
Securities to Be Held to Maturity:			
Security	E	$ 970,000	$ 980,000
	F	412,000	409,000
Totals		$1,382,000	$1,389,000

No investments were sold during 2000. All securities except Security D and Security F are considered short-term investments. None of the market changes is considered permanent.

Required:
Determine the following amounts at December 31, 2000:

1. Investments reported as current assets.
2. Investments reported as noncurrent assets.
3. Unrealized gain (or loss) component of income before taxes.
4. Unrealized gain (or loss) component of shareholders' equity.

Exercise 12-3
Equity method; purchase; investee income; dividends

As a long-term investment at the beginning of the fiscal year, Paper Products International purchased 35% of Reed's Restaurant Supplies, Inc.'s 12 million shares for $73 million. The fair value and book value of the shares were the same at that time. During the year, Reed's Restaurant Supplies earned net income of $20 million and distributed cash dividends of $1.10 per share. At the end of the year, the fair value of the shares is $59 million.

Required:
Prepare the appropriate journal entries from the purchase through the end of the year.

Exercise 12-4
Equity method: adjustments for depreciation and goodwill

J & W Leasing paid $76 million on January 4, 2000, for 5 million shares of Conley Trucks common stock. The investment represents a 25% interest in the net assets of Conley and gave J & W the ability to exercise significant influence over Conley's operations. J & W received dividends of $1.20 per share on December 27, 2000, and Conley reported net income of $60 million for the year ended December 31, 2000. The market value of Conley's common stock at December 31, 2000, was $22.25 per share.

- The book value of Conley's net assets was $212 million.
- The fair market value of Conley's depreciable assets exceeded their book value by $40 million. These assets had an average remaining useful life of 5 years.
- The remainder of the excess of the cost of the investment over the book value of net assets purchased was attributable to goodwill to be amortized over 10 years.

Required:
Prepare all appropriate journal entries related to the investment during 2000.

PROBLEMS

Problem 12-1
Investment securities and equity method investments compared

On January 4, 2000, RTN Industries paid $648,000 for 20,000 shares of Austin Cattle Company common stock. The investment represents a 30% interest in the net assets of Austin and gave RTN the ability to exercise significant influence over Austin's operations. RTN received dividends of $3.00 per share on December 6, 2000, and Austin reported net income of $320,000 for the year ended December 31, 2000. The market value of Austin's common stock at December 31, 2000, was $32 per share. The book value of Austin's net assets was $1,600,000 and:

a. The fair market value of Austin's depreciable assets, with an average remaining useful life of 8 years, exceeded their book value by $160,000.
b. The remainder of the excess of the cost of the investment over the book value of net assets purchased was attributable to goodwill to be amortized over 10 years.

Required:
1. Prepare all appropriate journal entries related to the investment during 2000, assuming RTN accounts for this investment by the equity method.
2. Prepare the journal entries required by RTN, assuming that the 20,000 shares represents a 10%interest in the net assets of Austin rather than a 30% interest.

Problem 12-2
Equity method

Southeast Pulp and Paper, a paper and allied products manufacturer, was seeking to gain a foothold in Mexico. Toward that end, the company bought 40% of the outstanding common shares of Monterrey Milling, Inc. on January 3, 2000, for $80 million.

At the date of purchase, the book value of Monterrey's net assets was $155 million. The book values and fair values for all balance sheet items were the same except for inventory and plant facilities. The fair value exceeded book value by $1 million for the inventory and by $4 million for the plant facilities.

The estimated useful life of the plant facilities is 8 years. Goodwill, if any, is to be amortized by Southeast over 10 years. All inventory acquired was sold during 2000.

Monterrey reported net income of $28 million for the year ended December 31, 2000. Monterrey paid a cash dividend of $6 million.

Required:

1. Prepare all appropriate journal entries related to the investment during 2000.
2. What amount should Southeast report as its income from its investment in Monterrey for the year ended December 31, 2000?
3. What amount should Southeast report on its balance sheet as its investment in Monterrey?
4. What should Southeast report on its statement of cash flows regarding its investment in Monterrey?

EXERCISES

Exercise 13-1
Bank loan; accrued interest

On September 1, 2000, Tri-State Paving Inc., an asphalt resurfacing and repairing company, borrowed $6 million cash to fund a twenty mile highway project. The loan was made by Alabama TrustCorp under a noncommitted short-term line of credit arrangement. Tri-State issued a 6-month, 14% promissory note. Interest was payable at maturity. Tri-State's fiscal period is the calendar year.

Required:
1. Prepare the journal entry for the issuance of the note by Tri-State Paving Inc.
2. Prepare the appropriate adjusting entry for the note by Tri-State on December 31, 2000.
3. Prepare the journal entry for the payment of the note at maturity.

Exercise 13-2
Determining accrued interest in various situations

On May 1, 2000, Ex-Cel Industries issued 9-month notes in the amount of $300 million. Interest is payable at maturity.

Required:
Determine the amount of interest expense that should be recorded in a year-end adjusting entry under each of the following independent assumptions:

	Interest rate	Fiscal Year End
1.	13%	December 31
2.	10%	October 31
3.	9%	June 30
4.	7%	January 31

Exercise 13-3
Short-term notes

The following selected transactions relate to liabilities of Odyssey Travel Corporation. Odyssey's fiscal year ends on December 31.

Required:
Prepare the appropriate journal entries through the maturity of each liability.

2000

Jan. 22	Negotiated a revolving credit agreement with Massey Bank which can be renewed annually upon bank approval. The amount available under the line of credit is $6,000,000 at the bank's prime rate.
Mar. 1	Arranged a 3-month bank loan of $7 million with Massey Bank under the line of credit agreement. Interest at the prime rate of 10% was payable at maturity.
June 1	Paid the 10% note at maturity.
Nov. 1	Supported by the credit line, issued $6 million of commercial paper on a nine-month note. Interest was discounted at issuance at a 8% discount rate.
Dec. 31	Recorded any necessary adjusting entry(s).

2001

Aug. 1	Paid the commercial paper at maturity.

Exercise 13-4
Current – noncurrent classification of debt

At December 31, 2000, Parker Petroleum's liabilities include the following:

1. $22 million of 10% notes are due on March 31, 2005. A debt covenant requires Parker to maintain current assets at least equal to 150% of its current liabilities. On December 31, 2000, Parker is in violation of this covenant. Parker obtained a waiver from City Corp Bank until June 2001, having convinced the bank that the company's normal 2 to 1 ratio of current assets to current liabilities will be reestablished during the first half of 2001.
2. $9 million of noncallable 13% bonds were issued for $9 million on September 30, 1969. The bonds mature on August 31, 2001. Sufficient cash is expected to be available to retire the bonds at maturity.
3. $15 million of 10% bonds were issued for $15 million on June 30, 1980. The bonds mature on June 30, 2010, but bondholders have the option of calling (demanding payment on) the bonds on June 30, 2001. However, the call option is not expected to be exercised, given prevailing market conditions.

Required:
What portion of the debt can be excluded from classification as a current liability (that is, reported as a noncurrent liability)? Explain.

Exercise 13-5
Warranties

Safe-Loc Security Door Corp. introduced a new line of commercial security doors in 2000 that carry a four-year warranty against manufacturer's defects. Based on their experience with previous product introductions, warranty costs are expected to approximate 4% of sales. Sales and actual warranty expenditures for the first year of selling the product were:

Sales	Actual warranty expenditures
$7,500,000	$124,800

Required:
1. Does this situation represent a loss contingency? Why or why not? How should it be accounted for?
2. Prepare journal entries that summarize sales of the security doors (assume all credit sales) and any aspects of the warranty that should be recorded during 2000.
3. What amount should Safe-Loc report as a liability at December 31, 2000?

PROBLEMS

Problem 13-1
Bank loan: accrued interest

Blanton Plastics, a household plastic product manufacturer, borrowed $14 million cash on October 1, 1997, to provide working capital for year-end production. Blanton issued a 4-month, 12% promissory note to N,C&I Bank under a prearranged short-term line of credit. Interest on the note was payable at maturity. Each firm's fiscal period is the calendar year.

Required:

1. Prepare the journal entries to record (a) the issuance of the note by Blanton Plastics and (b) N,C&I Bank's receivable on October 1, 1997.
2. Prepare the journal entries by both firms to record all subsequent events related to the note through January 31, 1998.
3. Suppose the face amount of the note was adjusted to include interest (a noninterest-bearing note) and 12% is the bank's stated "discount rate." Prepare the journal entries to record the issuance of the noninterest-bearing note by Blanton Plastics on October 1, 1997. What would be the effective interest rate?

Problem 13-2
Various contingencies

Eastern Manufacturing is involved with several situations that possibly involve contingencies. Each is described below. Eastern's fiscal year ends December 31, and the 1997 financial statements are issued on March 15, 1998.

1. Eastern is involved in a lawsuit resulting from a dispute with a supplier. On February 3, 1998, judgment was rendered against Eastern in the amount of $107 million plus interest, a total of $122 million. Eastern plans to appeal the judgment and is unable to predict its outcome though it is not expected to have a material adverse effect on the company.
2. In November, 1996, the State of Nevada filed suit against Eastern, seeking civil penalties and injunctive relief for violations of environmental laws regulating hazardous waste. On January 12, 1998, Eastern reached a settlement with state authorities. Based upon discussions with legal counsel, the Company feels it is probable that $140 million will be required to cover the cost of violations. Eastern believes that the ultimate settlement of this claim will not have a material adverse effect on the company.
3. Eastern is the plaintiff in a $200 million lawsuit filed against United Steel for damages due to lost profits from rejected contracts and for unpaid receivables. The case is in final appeal and legal counsel advises that it is probable that Eastern will prevail and be awarded $100 million.
4. At March 15, 1998, the IRS is in the process of auditing Eastern's tax returns for 1995-1997, but has not proposed a deficiency assessment. Management feels an assessment is reasonably possible, and if an assessment is made an unfavorable settlement of up to $33 million is reasonably possible.

Required:

1. Determine the appropriate means of reporting each situation. Explain your reasoning.
2. Prepare any necessary journal entries and disclosure notes.

Problem 13-3
Various contingencies

Western Manufacturing is involved with several situations that possibly involve contingencies. Each is described below. Western's fiscal year is the calendar year 1997, and the 1997 financial statements are issued on March 15, 1998.

1. During 1997, Western experienced labor disputes at three of its plants. Management hopes an agreement will soon be reached. However negotiations between the Company and the unions have not produced an acceptable settlement and, as a result, strikes are ongoing at these facilities since March 1, 1998. It is virtually certain that material costs will be incurred but the amount of possible costs cannot be reasonably ascertained.
2. In accordance with a 1995 contractual agreement with A.J. Conner Company, Western is entitled to $37 million for certain fees and expense reimbursements. These were written off as bad debts in 1996. A.J. Conner has filed for bankruptcy. The bankruptcy court on February 4, 1998, ordered A.J. Conner to pay $23 million immediately upon consummation of a proposed merger with Garner Holding Group.
3. Western warrants most products it sells against defects in materials and workmanship for a period of a year. Based on their experience with previous product introductions, warranty costs are expected to approximate 2% of sales. A warranty liability of $39 million was reported at December 31, 1996. Sales of warranted products during 1997 were $2,100 million and actual warranty expenditures were $40 million. Expenditures in excess of the existing liability were debited to warranty expense.
4. Western is involved in a suit filed in January 1998 by Crump Holdings seeking $88 million, as an adjustment to the purchase price in connection with the Company's sale of its textile business in 1997. The suit alleges that Western misstated the assets and liabilities used to calculate the purchase price for the textile division. Legal counsel advises that it is reasonably possible that Western could end up losing an indeterminable but material amount not expected to have a material adverse effect on the Company's financial position.

Required:

1. Determine the appropriate means of reporting each situation. Explain your reasoning.
2. Prepare any necessary journal entries and disclosure notes.

EXERCISES

Exercise 14-1
Accrued interest

On March 1, 2000, CMT Corporation issued $50 million of 12% bonds, dated January 1, 2000, for $47 million (plus accrued interest). The bonds mature on December 31, 2019, and pay interest semiannually on June 30 and December 31. CMT's fiscal period is the calendar year.

Required:
1. Determine the amount of accrued interest that was included in the proceeds received from the bond sale.
2. Prepare the journal entry for the issuance of the bonds by CMT.

Exercise 14-2
Determine the price of bonds; issuance; effective interest; no amortization schedule

Ticket, Inc. issued 10% bonds, dated January 1, with a face amount of $240 million on January 1, 2000. The bonds mature in 2010 (10 years). For bonds of similar risk and maturity the market yield is 12%. Interest is paid semiannually on June 30 and December 31.

Required:
1. Determine the price of the bonds at January 1, 2000.
2. Prepare the journal entry to record their issuance by Ticket on January 1, 2000.
3. Prepare the journal entry to record interest on June 30, 2000 (at the effective rate). [Do not prepare an amortization schedule.]
4. Prepare the journal entry to record interest on December 31, 2000 (at the effective rate). [Do not prepare an amortization schedule.]

Exercise 14-3
Convertible bonds

On January 1, 2000, Schmidt Security issued $60 million of 9%, 10-year convertible bonds at 102. The bonds pay interest on June 30 and December 31. Each $1,000 bond is convertible into 40 shares of Schmidt's $1 par common stock. Facial Mapping Company purchased 10% of the issue as an investment.

Required:
1. Prepare the journal entries for the issuance of the bonds by Schmidt and the purchase of the bond investment by Facial Mapping.
2. Prepare the journal entries for the June 30, 2004, interest payment by both Schmidt and Facial Mapping assuming both use the straight-line method.
3. On July 1, 2005, when Schmidt's common stock had a market price of $33 per share, Facial Mapping converted the bonds it held. Prepare the journal entries by both Schmidt and Facial Mapping for the conversion of the bonds (book value method).

PROBLEMS

Problem 14-1
Straight-line and effective interest compared

On January 1, 2000, Lamb Services issued $200,000, 9%, four-year bonds. Interest is paid semiannually on June 30 and December 31. The bonds were issued at $193,537 to yield an annual return of 10%.

Required:

1. Prepare an amortization schedule that determines interest at the effective interest rate.
2. Prepare an amortization schedule by the straight-line method.
3. Prepare the journal entries to record interest expense on June 30, 2002, by each of the two approaches.
4. Explain why the pattern of interest differs between the two methods.
5. Assuming the market rate is still 10%, what price would a second investor pay the first investor on June 30, 2002, for $20,000 of the bonds?

Problem 14-2
Note and installment note with unrealistic interest rate

Warren Machinery, Inc. constructed an industrial lathe for Nelson Equipment that was completed and ready for use on January 1, 2000. Nelson paid for the conveyor by issuing a $500,000, 4-year note that specified 5% interest to be paid on December 31 of each year. The conveyor was custom-built for Nelson so its cash price was unknown. By comparison with similar transactions it was determined that a reasonable interest rate was 10%.

Required:

1. Prepare the journal entry for Nelson's purchase of the conveyor on January 1, 2000.
2. Prepare an amortization schedule for the four-year term of the note.
3. Prepare the journal entry for Nelson's third interest payment on December 31, 2002.
4. If Nelson's note had been an installment note to be paid in four equal payments at the end of each year beginning December 31, 2000, what would be the amount of each installment?
5. Prepare an amortization schedule for the four-year term of the installment note.
6. Prepare the journal entry for Nelson's third installment payment on December 31, 2002.

Problem 14-3
Early extinguishment

The long-term liability section of Westin Laboratories balance sheet as of December 31, 1999, included 10% bonds having a face amount of $200 million and a remaining premium of $30 million. On January 1, 2000, Eastern Post retired some of the bonds before their scheduled maturity.

Required:
Prepare the journal entry by Westin to record the redemption of the bonds under each of the independent circumstances below:
1. Westin called half the bonds at the call price of 102 (102% of face amount).
2. Westin repurchased $50 million of the bonds on the open market at their market price of $52.5 million.

Problem 14-4
Troubled debt restructuring

At January 1, 2000, Banyon, Inc. was indebted to Security Bank under a $60 million, 10% unsecured note. The note was signed January 1, 1994, and was due December 31, 2003. Annual interest was last paid on December 31, 1998. Banyon was experiencing severe financial difficulties and negotiated a restructuring of the terms of the debt agreement.

Required:
Prepare all journal entries by Banyon, Inc. to record the restructuring and any remaining transactions relating to the debt under each of the independent circumstances below:
1. Security Bank agreed to settle the debt in exchange for land having a fair market value of $48 million, but carried on Banyon 's books at $39 million.
2. Security Bank agreed to (a) forgive the interest accrued from last year, (b) reduce the remaining four interest payments to $3 million each, and (c) reduce the principal to $45 million.
3. Security Bank agreed to defer all payments (including accrued interest) until the maturity date and accept $83,325,000 at that time in settlement of the debt.

EXERCISES

Exercise 15-1
Operating Lease

On January 1, 2000, Gothic Corporation, an internet training firm, leased several computers from HardWhere Inc. under a 3-year operating lease agreement. The contract calls for four rent payments of $40,000 each, payable semiannually on June 30 and December 31 each year. The computers were acquired by HardWhere at a cost of $350,000 and were expected to have a useful life of 5 years with no residual value.

Required:
Prepare the appropriate entries for both (a) the lessee and (b) the lessor from the inception of the lease through the end of 2000. (Use straight-line depreciation.)

Exercise 15-2
Capital lease; lessee

[Note: Exercises 2, 3, and 4 are three variations of the same basic situation.]
Manufacturers Eastern leased high-tech electronic equipment from Franklin Leasing on January 1, 2000. Franklin purchased the equipment from National Machines at a cost of $107,866.

Related information:

Lease term	3 years (12 quarterly periods)
Quarterly rental payments	$10,000 - beginning of each period
Economic life of asset	3 years
Fair value of asset	$107,866
Implicit interest rate	8%
(Also lessee's incremental borrowing rate)	

Required:
Prepare a lease amortization schedule and appropriate entries for Manufacturers Eastern from the inception of the lease through January 1, 2001. Depreciation is recorded at the end of each fiscal year (December 31) on a straight-line basis.

Exercise 15-3
Direct financing lease; lessor

[Note: Exercises 2, 3, and 4 are three variations of the same basic situation.]
Franklin Leasing leased high-tech electronic equipment to Manufacturers Eastern on January 1, 2000. Franklin purchased the equipment from National Machines at a cost of $107,866.

Related information:

Lease term	3 years (12 quarterly periods)
Quarterly rental payments	$10,000 - beginning of each period
Economic life of asset	3 years
Fair value of asset	$107,866
Implicit interest rate	8%
(Also lessee's incremental borrowing rate)	

Required:
Prepare a lease amortization schedule and appropriate entries for Franklin Leasing from the inception of the lease through January 1, 2001. Franklin's fiscal year ends December 31.

Exercise 15-4
Sales-type lease: lessor

[Note: Exercises 2, 3, and 4 are three variations of the same basic situation.]

Manufacturers Eastern leased high-tech electronic equipment from National Machines on January 1, 2000. National Machines manufactured the equipment at a cost of $90,000.

Related information:

Lease term	3 years (12 quarterly periods)
Quarterly rental payments	$10,000 - beginning of each period
Economic life of asset	3 years
Fair value of asset	$107,866
Implicit interest rate	8%
(Also lessee's incremental borrowing rate)	

Required:

1. Show how National Machines determined the $10,000 quarterly rental payments.
2. Prepare appropriate entries for National Machines to record the lease at its inception, January 1, 2000, and the second rental payment on April 1, 2000.

Exercise 15-5
Sale-leaseback; capital lease

To raise operating funds, WSMM Broadcasting sold a helicopter used in news reports on January 1, 2000, to a finance company for $1,540,000. WSMM immediately leased the helicopter back for a 13-year period, at which time ownership of the helicopter will transfer to WSMM. The helicopter has a fair value of $1,600,000. Its cost and its carrying value were $1,240,000. Its useful life is estimated to be 20 years. The lease requires WSMM to make payments of $205,542 to the finance company each January 1. WSMM depreciates assets on a straight-line basis. The lease has an implicit rate of 11%.

Required:

Prepare the appropriate entries for WSMM on (a) January 1, 2000, to record the sale-leaseback and (b) December 31, 2000, to record necessary adjustments.

PROBLEMS

Problem 15-1
Direct financing and sales-type lease; lessee and lessor

Tech-Knowledgies develops and manufactures voice recognition hardware. Star Leasing purchased a voice recognition hardware from Tech-Knowledgies for $500,000 and leased it to Pal Learning Systems on January 1, 2000.

Lease description:

Quarterly rental payments	$32,629 - beginning of each period
Lease term	5 years (20 quarters)
No residual value; no BPO	
Economic life of lithotripter	5 years
Implicit interest rate and lessee's incremental borrowing rate	12%
Fair value of asset	$500,000

Collectibility of the rental payments is reasonably assured, and there are no lessor costs yet to be incurred.

Required:

1. How should this lease be classified by Pal Learning Systems and by Star Leasing?
2. Prepare appropriate entries for both Pal Learning Systems and Star Leasing from the inception of the lease through the second rental payment on April 1, 2000. Depreciation is recorded at the end of each fiscal year (December 31).
3. Assume Pal Learning Systems leased the hardware directly from the manufacturer, Tech-Knowledgies, which produced the machine at a cost of $450,000. Prepare appropriate entries for Tech-Knowledgies from the inception of the lease through the second rental payment on April 1, 2000.

Problem 15-2
Guaranteed residual value; direct financing lease

On December 31, 2000, HHH Corp. leased equipment to Blair Co. for a 4-year period ending December 31, 2005, at which time possession of the leased asset will revert back to HHH Corp. The equipment cost HHH Corp. $1,097,280 and has an expected useful life of 6 years. Its normal sales price is $1,097,280. The lessee-guaranteed residual value at December 31, 2005, is $75,000. Equal payments under the lease are $300,000 and are due on December 31 of each year. The first payment was made on December 31, 2000. Collectability of the remaining lease payments is reasonably assured, and HHH Corp. has no material cost uncertainties. Blair's incremental borrowing rate is 12%. Blair knows the interest rate implicit in the lease payments is 10%. Both companies use straight-line depreciation.

Required:

1. Show how HHH Corp. calculated the $300,000 annual rental payments.
2. How should this lease be classified (a) by Blair Co. (the lessee) and (b) by HHH Corp. (the lessor)? Why?
3. Prepare the appropriate entries for both Blair Co. and HHH Corp. on December 31, 2000.
4. Prepare an amortization schedule(s) that describes the pattern of interest over the lease term for the lessee and the lessor.
5. Prepare all appropriate entries for both Blair and HHH Corp. on December 31, 2001 (the second rent payment and depreciation).
6. Prepare the appropriate entries for both Blair and HHH Corp. on December 31, 2001 (the end of the lease), assuming the equipment is returned to HHH Corp. and the actual residual value on that date is $4,500.

EXERCISES

Exercise 16-1
Single temporary difference; taxable income given

Stancil Industries reports *pretax accounting income* of $80 million, but due to a single temporary difference, *taxable income* is only $50 million. At the beginning of the year, no temporary differences existed.

Required:
Assuming a tax rate of 35%, prepare the appropriate journal entry to record Stancil's income taxes.

Exercise 16-2
Single temporary difference; income tax payable given

In 2000, Lambert Services collected rent revenue for 2001 tenant occupancy. For income tax reporting, the rent is taxed when collected. For financial statement reporting, the rent is recognized as income in the period earned. The unearned portion of the rent collected in 2000 amounted to $90,000 at December 31, 2000. Lambert had no temporary differences at the beginning of the year.

Required:
Assuming an income tax rate of 40%, and that the 2000 income tax payable is $285,000, prepare the journal entry to record income taxes for 2000.

Exercise 16-3
Deferred tax asset; income tax payable given; previous balance in valuation allowance

At the end of 1999, Mathis Industries had a deferred tax asset account with a balance of $120 million attributable to a temporary book-tax difference of $300 million in a liability for estimated expenses. At the end of 2000, the temporary difference is $280 million. Mathis has no other temporary differences. Taxable income for 2000 is $720 million and the tax rate is 40%.

Mathis has a valuation allowance of $40 million for the deferred tax asset at the beginning of 2000.

Required:
1. Prepare the journal entry(s) to record Mathis's income taxes for 2000 assuming it is "more likely than not" that the deferred tax asset will be realized.
2. Prepare the journal entry(s) to record Mathis's income taxes for 2000 assuming it is "more likely than not" that one-half of the deferred tax asset will not ultimately be realized.

Exercise 16-4
Single temporary difference; non-temporary difference; calculate taxable income

Fessler Transport began operations in January 2000, and purchased a delivery truck for $160,000.

Fessler plans to use straight-line depreciation over a four-year expected useful life for financial reporting purposes. For tax purposes, the deduction is 50% of cost in 2000, 30% in 2001, and 20% in 2002. Pretax accounting income for 2000 was $900,000, which includes interest revenue of $160,000 from municipal bonds. The enacted tax rate is 40%.

Required:

Assuming no differences between accounting income and taxable income other than those described above:

1. Prepare the journal entry to record income taxes in 2000.
2. What is Fessler's 2000 net income?

Exercise 16-5
Intraperiod tax allocation

The following income statement does not reflect intraperiod tax allocation.

Income Statement
For the fiscal year ended June 30, 2000

	($ in millions)
Revenues	$415
Cost of goods sold	(175)
Gross profit	$240
Operating expenses	(90)
Income tax expense	(42)
Income before extraordinary item and cumulative effect of accounting change	$108
Extraordinary casualty loss	(5)
Cumulative effect of change in depreciation methods	(40)
Net income	$ 63

The company's tax rate is 40%.

Required:
Recast the income statement to reflect intraperiod tax allocation.

PROBLEMS

Problem 16-1
Change in tax rate; single temporary difference

Commercial Development began operations in December 2000. When lots for industrial development are sold, Commercial recognizes income for financial reporting purposes in the year of the sale. For some lots, Commercial recognizes income for tax purposes when collected. Income recognized for financial reporting purposes in 2000 for lots sold this way was $48 million which will be collected over the next three years. Scheduled collections for 2001-2003 are as follows:

2001	$ 16 million
2002	20 million
2003	12 million
	$48 million

Pretax *accounting* income for 2000 was $68 million. The enacted tax rate is 40 percent.

Required:

1. Assuming no differences between accounting income and taxable income other than those described above, prepare the journal entry to record income taxes in 2000.
2. Suppose a new tax law, revising the tax rate from 40% to 35%, beginning in 2001, is *enacted in 2001*, when pretax accounting income was $60 million. Prepare the appropriate journal entry to record income taxes in 2001.
3. If the new tax rate had not been enacted, what would have been the appropriate balance in the deferred tax liability account at the end of 2001? Why?

Problem 16-2
Operating loss carryback and carryforward; temporary difference; non-temporary difference

CPS Corporation reported a pretax operating loss of $540,000 for financial reporting purposes in 2000. Contributing to the loss were (a) a penalty of $20,000 assessed by the Environmental Protection Agency for violation of a federal law and paid in 2000 and (b) an estimated loss of $40,000 from accruing a loss contingency. The loss will be tax deductible when paid in 2001.

The enacted tax rate is 40%. There were no temporary differences at the beginning of the year and none originating in 2000 other than those described above. Taxable income in CPS's two previous years of operation was as follows:

1998	300,000
1999	120,000

Required:

1. Prepare the journal entry to recognize the income tax benefit of the operating loss in 2000. CPS elects the carryback option.
2. Show the lower portion of the 2000 income statement that reports the income tax benefit of the operating loss.
3. Prepare the journal entry to record income taxes in 2001 assuming pretax accounting income is $240,000. No additional temporary differences originate in 2001.

EXERCISES

Exercise 17-1
Determine pension expense

Hunt Industries has a noncontributory, defined benefit pension plan. At December 31, 2000, Hunt received the following information:

Projected Benefit obligation	($ in millions)
Balance, January 1	$360
Service cost	60
Interest cost	36
Benefits paid	(27)
Balance, December 31	$429
Plan Assets	
Balance, January 1	$240
Actual return on plan assets	27
Contributions 2000	60
Benefits paid	(27)
Balance, December 31	$300

The expected long-term rate of return on plan assets was 10%. There was no unrecognized prior service cost, gains and losses, or transition cost on January 1, 2000.

Required:

1. Determine Hunt's pension expense for 2000.
2. Prepare the journal entry to record Hunt's pension expense and funding for 2000.

Exercise 17-2
Minimum liability

C&D Consulting has a defined benefit pension plan. C&D's policy is to fund the plan annually, cash payments being made at the end of each year. Data relating to the pension plan for 2000 are as follows:

	($ in millions)
Prepaid (accrued) pension cost at the beginning of the year – debit balance	$ 40
Net pension expense for 2000	200
Unrecognized prior service cost at year end	150
Accumulated benefit obligation at year end	585
Projected benefit obligation at year end	700
Fair value of plan assets at year end	520
Payment to trustee at year end	190

Required:
Determine C&D's pension liability to be reported on the 2000 balance sheet and prepare any journal entry necessary to achieve that reporting objective.

PROBLEMS

Problem 17-1
ABO calculations: present value concepts

[Problems 1 – 5 are variations of the same situation, designed to focus on different elements of the pension plan.]

D&C Advisory's defined benefit pension plan specifies annual retirement benefits equal to: 1.5% x service years x final year's salary, payable at the end of each year. Bobby Flay was hired by D&C at the beginning of 1986 and is expected to retire at the end of 2030 after 45 years service. His retirement is expected to span 18 years. Flay's salary is $80,000 at the end of 2000, and the company's actuary projects his salary to be $250,000 at retirement. The actuary's discount rate is 7%.

Required:

1. Draw a time line that depicts Flay's expected service period, retirement period, and a 2000 measurement date for the pension obligation.
2. Estimate by the accumulated benefits approach the amount of Flay's annual retirement payments earned as of the end of 2000.
3. What is the company's accumulated benefit obligation at the end of 2000 with respect to Flay?
4. If no estimates are changed in the meantime, what will be the accumulated benefit obligation at the end of 2002 (two years later) when Flay's salary is $85,000?

Problem 17-2
PBO calculations; present value concepts

[Problems 1 – 5 are variations of the same situation, designed to focus on different elements of the pension plan.]

D&C Advisory's defined benefit pension plan specifies annual retirement benefits equal to: 1.5% x service years x final year's salary, payable at the end of each year. Bobby Flay was hired by D&C at the beginning of 1986 and is expected to retire at the end of 2030 after 45 years service. His retirement is expected to span 18 years. Flay's salary is $80,000 at the end of 2000, and the company's actuary projects his salary to be $250,000 at retirement. The actuary's discount rate is 7%.

Required:

1. Draw a time line that depicts Flay's expected service period, retirement period, and a 2000 measurement date for the pension obligation.
2. Estimate by the projected benefits approach the amount of Flay's annual retirement payments earned as of the end of 2000.
3. What is the company's projected benefit obligation at the end of 2000 with respect to Flay?
4. If no estimates are changed in the meantime, what will be the projected benefit obligation at the end of 2002 (two years later) when Flay's salary is $85,000?

Problem 17-3
Service cost, interest, and PBO calculations; present value concepts

[Problems 1 – 5 are variations of the same situation, designed to focus on different elements of the pension plan.]

D&C Advisory's defined benefit pension plan specifies annual retirement benefits equal to: 1.5% x service years x final year's salary, payable at the end of each year. Bobby Flay was hired by D&C at the beginning of 1986 and is expected to retire at the end of 2030 after 45 years service. His retirement is expected to span 18 years. Flay's salary is $80,000 at the end of 2000, and the company's actuary projects his salary to be $250,000 at retirement. The actuary's discount rate is 7%.

Required:

1. What is the company's projected benefit obligation at the *beginning* of 2000 (after 14 years' service) with respect to Flay?
2. Estimate by the projected benefits approach the portion of Flay's annual retirement payments attributable to 2000 service.
3. What is the company's service cost for 2000 with respect to Flay?
4. What is the company's interest cost for 2000 with respect to Flay?
5. Combine your answers to requirements 1, 3, and 4 to determine the company's projected benefit obligation at the *end* of 2000 (after 15 years' service) with respect to Flay?

Problem 17-4
Prior service cost; components of pension expense; present value concepts

[Problems 1 – 5 are variations of the same situation, designed to focus on different elements of the pension plan.]

D&C Advisory's defined benefit pension plan specifies annual retirement benefits equal to: 1.5% x service years x final year's salary, payable at the end of each year. Bobby Flay was hired by D&C at the beginning of 1986 and is expected to retire at the end of 2030 after 45 years service. His retirement is expected to span 18 years. Flay's salary is $80,000 at the end of 2000, and the company's actuary projects his salary to be $250,000 at retirement. The actuary's discount rate is 7%.

At the beginning of 2001, the pension formula was amended to:

1.65% x service years x final year's salary

The amendment was made retroactive to apply the increased benefits to prior service years.

Required:

1. What is the company's prior service cost at the beginning of 2001 with respect to Flay after the amendment described above?
2. Since the amendment occurred at the *beginning* of 2001, amortization of the prior service cost begins in 2001. What is the prior service cost amortization that would be included in pension expense?
3. What is the service cost for 2001 with respect to Flay?
4. What is the interest cost for 2001 with respect to Flay?
5. Calculate pension expense for 2001 with respect to Flay assuming plan assets attributable to him of $170,000 and a rate of return (actual and expected) of 10%.

Problem 17-5
Loss on PBO; present value concepts

[Problems 1 – 5 are variations of the same situation, designed to focus on different elements of the pension plan.]

D&C Advisory's defined benefit pension plan specifies annual retirement benefits equal to: 1.5% x service years x final year's salary, payable at the end of each year. Bobby Flay was hired by D&C at the beginning of 1986 and is expected to retire at the end of 2030 after 45 years service. His retirement is expected to span 18 years. Flay's salary is $80,000 at the end of 2000, and the company's actuary projects his salary to be $250,000 at retirement. The actuary's discount rate is 7%.

At the beginning of 2001, changing economic conditions caused the actuary to reassess the applicable discount rate. It was decided that 6% is the appropriate rate.

Required:

Calculate the effect of the change in the assumed discount rate on the PBO at the beginning of 2001 with respect to Flay.

EXERCISES

Exercise 18-1
Postretirement benefits; determine the APBO and service cost

Love Industries has an unfunded postretirement health care benefit plan. Medical care benefits are provided to employees who render 10 years service and attain age 57 while in service. At the end of 2000, Larry Abbott is 31. He was hired by Love at age 27 (6 years ago) and is expected to retire at age 64. The expected postretirement benefit obligation for Lukawitz at the end of 2000 is $200,000 and $216,000 at the end of 2001.

Required:
Calculate the *accumulated postretirement benefit obligation* at the end of 2000 and 2001 and the *service cost* for 2000 and 2001 as pertaining to Abbott.

Exercise 18-2
Postretirement benefits; amortization of unrecognized transition obligation and prior service cost

Tomorrow, Inc. provides postretirement health care benefits to employees who provide at least 14 years service and reach age 61 while in service. On January 1, 2000, the following plan-related data were available:

	($ in millions)
Unrecognized transition obligation	$ 100
Accumulated postretirement benefit obligation	210
Fair value of plan assets	none
Average remaining service period to retirement	20 years
Average remaining service period to full eligibility	15 years

On January 1, 2000, Tomorrow amends the plan to provide certain dental benefits in addition to previously provided medical benefits. The actuary determines that the cost of making the amendment retroactive increases the APBO by $30 million. Management chooses to amortize the prior service cost on a straight-line basis. The service cost for 2000 is $61 million. The interest rate is 5%.

Required:
Calculate the postretirement benefit expense for 2000.

Exercise 18-3
Restricted stock award plan; forfeitures anticipated

LaRue Industries offers a variety of stock-based compensation plans to employees. Under its restricted stock award plan, the company on January 1, 2000, granted 12 million of its $1 par common shares to various regional managers. The shares are subject to forfeiture if employment is terminated within 3 years. The common shares have a market price of $25.50 per share on the grant date.

Required:
1. Determine the total compensation cost pertaining to the restricted shares.
2. Prepare the appropriate journal entry to record the award of restricted shares on January 1, 2000.
3. Prepare the appropriate journal entry to record compensation expense on December 31, 2000.
4. Suppose LaRue expected a 20% forfeiture rate on the restricted shares prior to vesting. Determine the total compensation cost, assuming the company chooses to follow the elective fair value approach for fixed compensation plans and chooses to anticipate forfeitures at the grant date.

Exercise 18-4
Stock option plan; elective fair value approach; forfeiture of options

On January 1, 2000, MEM Corporation granted 75,000 incentive stock options to branch managers, each permitting holders to purchase one share of the company's $1 par common shares within the next 7 years, but not before December 31, 2004 (the vesting date). The exercise price is the market price of the shares on the date of grant, currently $20 per share. The fair value of the options, estimated by an appropriate option pricing model, is $7 per option. MEM chooses to follow the elective fair value approach for fixed compensation plans.

Required:
1. Determine the total compensation cost pertaining to the options on January 1, 2000.
2. Prepare the appropriate journal entry to record compensation expense on December 31, 2000.
3. Unexpected turnover during 2001 caused the forfeiture of 10% of the stock options. Determine the adjusted compensation cost, and prepare the appropriate journal entry(s) on December 31, 2001.

Exercise 18-5
Stock appreciation rights; cash settlement

As part of its stock-based compensation package, National, Inc. granted 48,000 stock appreciation rights (SARs) to executives on January 1, 2000. At exercise, holders of the SARs are entitled to receive cash or stock equal in value to the excess of the market price at exercise over the share price at the date of grant. The SARs cannot be exercised until the end of 2002 (vesting date) and expire at the end of 2005. The common shares have a market price of $23 per share on the grant date. All recipients are expected to remain employed through the vesting date. The year-end share prices following the grant of the SARs are:

2000 – $25
2001 – $24
2002 – $25

Required:

1. Prepare the appropriate journal entry to record the award of SARs on January 1, 2000.
2. Prepare the appropriate journal entries pertaining to the SARs on December 31, 2000 – 2002.
3. The SARs are exercised on May 6, 2003, when the share price is $24, and executives choose to receive the market price appreciation in cash. Prepare the appropriate journal entry(ies) on that date.

EXERCISES

Exercise 19-1
Issuance of shares; noncash consideration

During its first year of operations, Yankee Communications entered into the following transactions relating to shareholders' equity. The articles of incorporation authorized the issue of 240 million common shares, $1 par per share, and 30 million preferred shares, $50 par per share.

Required:
Prepare the appropriate journal entries to record each transaction:

February 13	Sold 60 million common shares, for $10 per share.
February 14	Issued 1 million common shares to attorneys in exchange for legal services.
February 14	Sold 3 million of its common shares and 1 million preferred shares for $60 million.
November 16	Issued 190,000 of its common shares in exchange for equipment for which the cash price was known to be $1,844,000.

Exercise 19-2
Retirement of shares

Brand Storage Company's articles of incorporation authorized the issuance of 520 million common shares. The transactions described below effected changes in Brand's outstanding shares. Prior to the transactions, Brand's shareholders' equity included the following:

Shareholders' Equity	$ in millions
Common stock, 400 million shares at $1 par, ...	$400
Paid-in capital – excess of par	1,200
Retained earnings	84

Required:
Assuming that Brand Communications retires shares it reacquires (restores their status to that of authorized but unissued shares), record the appropriate journal entry for each of the following transactions:

a. On January 8, 2000, Brand reacquired 8 million shares at $6.00 per share.
b. On August 24, 2000, Brand reacquired 16 million shares at $5.50 per share.
c. On July 26, 2001, Brand sold 12 million common shares at $7.00 per share.

Exercise 19-3
Transactions affecting retained earnings

The balance sheet of MDS, Inc. included the following shareholders' equity accounts at December 31, 1999:

Paid-in capital:	
Preferred stock, 7.6%, 100,000 shares at $1 par	$ 100,000
Common stock, 728,000 shares at $1 par	728,000
Paid-in capital – excess of par, preferred	2,900,000
Paid-in capital – excess of par, common.........	5,148,000
Retained earnings..	9,800,000
Treasury stock, at cost; 8,000 common shares	(88,000)
Total shareholders' equity	$17,688,000

During 2000, several events and transactions affected the retained earnings of Consolidated Paper.

Required:

1. Prepare the appropriate entries for these events.
   a. On February 20, the board of directors declared a property dividend of 100,000 shares of Brown International common stock that MDS had been purchased in January as an investment (book value: $485,000). The investment shares had a fair market value of $5 per share and were distributed March 20 to shareholders of record February 28.
   b. On April 4, a 5 for 4 stock split was declared and distributed. The stock split was effected in the form of a 25% stock dividend. The market value of the $1 par common stock was $12 per share.
   c. On July 25, a 3% common stock dividend was declared and distributed. The market value of the common stock was $12 per share.
   d. On December 2, the board of directors declared the 7.6% cash dividend on the 100,000 preferred shares, payable on December 27 to shareholders of record December 19.
   e. On December 2, the board of directors declared a cash dividend of $.50 per share on its common shares, payable on December 27 to shareholders of record December 19.
2. Prepare the shareholders' equity section of the balance sheet for MDS, Inc. for the year ended at December 31, 2000. Net income for the year was $900,000.

PROBLEMS

Problem 19-1
Treasury stock – comparison of the cost and par value methods

The shareholders' equity section of the balance sheet of Dodge, Inc. included the following accounts at December 31, 1999:

Shareholders' Equity	$ in millions
Common stock, 80 million shares at $1 par, ...	$ 80
Paid-in capital – excess of par....................................	560
Paid-in capital – reacquired shares..............................	1
Retained earnings	350

Required:

1. During 2000, Dodge reacquired shares of its common stock to hold as treasury stock and later sold shares in two separate transactions. Prepare the entries for both the purchase and subsequent resale of treasury stock by both the *par value* and *cost* methods.
   a. On March 6, 2000, Dodge purchased 3 million shares of treasury stock at $10 per share.
   b. On September 3, 2000, the corporation sold 1 million shares of treasury stock at $11 per share.
   c. On October 12, 2002, the corporation sold 1 million shares of treasury stock at $4 per share.
2. Prepare the shareholders' equity section of Dodge's balance sheet at December 31, 2002, reporting treasury stock by both the *par value* and *cost* methods. Assume all net income earned in 2000-2002 was distributed to shareholders as cash dividends.

Problem 19-2
Shareholders' equity transactions; statement of shareholders' equity

Listed below are the transactions that affected the shareholders' equity of BLT Corporation during the period 2000 - 2002. At December 31, 1999, the corporation's accounts included:

	($ in 000s)
Common stock, 315 million shares at $1 par, ...	$315,000
Paid-in capital – excess of par....................................	1,890,000
Retained earnings..	2,910,000

a. November 2, 2000, the board of directors declared a cash dividend of $.80 per share on its common shares, payable to shareholders of record November 16, to be paid December 2.
b. On March 3, 2001, the board of directors declared a property dividend consisting of bonds of Blair County that BLT was holding as an investment. The bonds had a fair market value of $4.8 million, but were purchased two years previously for $3.9 million. Because they were intended to be held to maturity, the bonds had not been previously written up. The property dividend was payable to shareholders of record March 14, to be distributed April 6.
c. On July 13, 2001, the corporation declared and distributed a 5% common stock dividend (when the market value of the common stock was $21 per share). Cash was paid for fractional share rights representing 750,000 equivalent whole shares.
d. On November 2, 2001, the board of directors declared a cash dividend of $.80 per share on its common shares, payable to shareholders of record November 16, to be paid December 2.
e. On January 16, 2002, the board of directors declared and distributed a 3 for 2 stock split effected in the form of a 50% stock dividend when the market value of the common stock was $23 per share.
f. On November 2, 2002, the board of directors declared a cash dividend of $.65 per share on its common shares, payable to shareholders of record November 16, to be paid December 2.

Required:
1. Prepare the journal entries that BLT recorded during the three-year period for these transactions.
2. Prepare comparative statements of shareholders' equity for BLT for the three-year period ($ in 000s). Net income was $990 million, $1,185 million, and $1,365 million for 2000, 2001, and 2002, respectively.

Section 4

Additional Topics

EXERCISES

Exercise 20-1
Treasury stock; new shares; stock dividends; two years

The Reserve Company had 606 million shares of common stock outstanding at January 1, 2000. The following activities affected common shares during the year: There are no potentially dilutive securities outstanding.

2000
Feb. 27 Purchased 18 million shares of treasury stock.
Oct. 30 Sold the treasury shares purchased on February 27.
Nov. 29 Issued 72 million new shares.
Dec. 31 Net income for 2000 is $1,200 million.

2001
Jan. 14 Declared and issued a 2 for 1 stock split.
Dec. 31 Net income for 2001 is $1,200 million.

Required:
1. Determine the 2000 EPS.
2. Determine the 2001 EPS.
3. At what amount will the 2000 EPS be presented in the 2001 comparative financial statements?

PROBLEMS

Problem 20-1
Net loss; stock dividend; nonconvertible preferred stock; treasury shares; shares sold; extraordinary loss

On December 31, 1999, Parnell Corporation had 1,200,000 shares of common stock outstanding. Forty thousand shares of 7%, $100 par value cumulative, nonconvertible preferred stock were sold on January 2, 2000. On April 30, 2000, Parnell purchased 60,000 shares of its common stock as treasury stock. Twenty-four thousand treasury shares were sold on August 31. Parnell issued a 5% common stock dividend on June 12, 2000. No cash dividends were declared in 2000. For the year ended December 31, 2000, Parnell reported a net loss of $280,000, including an after-tax extraordinary loss of $800,000 from a litigation settlement.

Required:
1. Determine Parnell 's net loss per share for the year ended December 31, 2000.
2. Determine the per share amount of income or loss from continuing operations for the year ended December 31, 2000.
3. Prepare an EPS presentation that would be appropriate to appear on Ainsworth's 2000 and 1999 comparative income statements. Assume EPS were reported in 1999 as $.75, based on net income (no extraordinary items) of $900,000 and a weighted average number of common shares of 1,200,000.

Problem 20-2
Nonconvertible preferred stock; treasury shares; shares sold; stock dividend

On December 31, 1999, Warren Industries had 300 million shares of common stock and 2 million shares of 8%, noncumulative, nonconvertible preferred stock issued and outstanding. Warren issued a 4% common stock dividend on April 30 and paid cash dividends of $200 million and $39 million to common and preferred shareholders, respectively, on December 15, 2000.

On March 1, 2000, Warren sold 30 million common shares. In keeping with its long-term share repurchase plan, 2 million shares were retired on June 30. Warren's net income for the year ended December 31, 2000, was $1,050,000,000. The income tax rate is 40%.

Required:
Compute Warren 's earnings per share for the year ended December 31, 2000.

Problem 20-3
Nonconvertible preferred stock; treasury shares; shares sold; stock dividend; options; convertible bonds; contingently issuable shares

[Note: This is a variation of the previous problem, modified to include options, convertible bonds and contingently issuable shares.]

On December 31, 1999, Warren Industries had 300 million shares of common stock and 2 million shares of 8%, noncumulative, nonconvertible preferred stock issued and outstanding. Warren issued a 4% common stock dividend on April 30 and paid cash dividends of $200 million and $39 million to common and preferred shareholders, respectively, on December 15, 2000.

On March 1, 2000, Warren sold 30 million common shares. Also, as part of a 1999 agreement for the acquisition of RW, Inc., another 13 million shares (already adjusted for the stock dividend) are to be issued to former RW shareholders on December 31, 2001, if RW's 2001 net income is at least $250 million. In 2000, RW's net income was $290 million.

In keeping with its long-term share repurchase plan, 2 million shares were retired on June 30. Warren's net income for the year ended December 31, 2000, was $1,050,000,000. The income tax rate is 40%.

As part of an incentive compensation plan, Warren granted stock options to division managers at December 31 of the current and each of the previous two years. Each option permits its holder to buy one share of common stock at an exercise price equal to market value at the date of grant. Information concerning the number of options granted and common share prices follows:

Date granted	**Options granted** (adjusted for the stock dividend)	**Share price**
December 31, 1998	2 million	$34
December 31, 1999	4 million	$24
December 31, 2000	3 million	$30

The market price of the common stock averaged $32 per share during 2000.

On July 12, 1998, Warren issued $400 million of convertible 10% bonds at face value. Each $1,000 bond is convertible into 30 common shares (adjusted for the stock dividend).

Required:
Compute Warren's basic and diluted earnings per share for the year ended December 31, 2000.

Problem 20-4
Options; convertible preferred; additional shares

On January 1, 2000, Buffy Industries had outstanding 880 million common shares (par $1) that originally sold for $19 per share, and 8 million shares of 10% cumulative preferred stock (par $100), convertible into 80 million common shares.

On September 30, 2000, Buffy sold and issued an additional 32 million shares of common stock at $38. At December 31, 2000, there were common stock options outstanding, issued in 1999, and exercisable for 40 million shares of common stock at an exercise price of $30. The market price of the common stock at year-end was $48. During the year the price of the common shares had averaged $40.

Net income was $1,300,000,000. The tax rate for the year was 40%.

Required:
Compute basic and diluted EPS for the year ended December 31, 2000.

EXERCISES

Exercise 21-1
Change in accounting principle; change in depreciation methods

Bearing Products bought a machine at a total cost of $105,000 million in 1997. The machine was being depreciated over a 10-year life using the sum-of-the-years'-digits method. The residual value is expected to be $6,000. At the beginning of 2000 Bearing decided to change to the straight-line method.

Required:
Prepare all appropriate journal entry(s) relating to the machine for 2000. (Ignore income tax effects.)

Exercise 21-2
Change in inventory costing methods

In 2001, the Emerson, Inc. changed its method of valuing inventory from the FIFO method to the average cost method. At December 31, 2000, Emerson's inventories were $96,000 (FIFO). Emerson's records indicated that the inventories would have totaled $71,400 at December 31, 2000, if determined on an average cost basis.

Required:
1. Prepare the journal entry to record the adjustment. (Ignore income taxes.)
2. Briefly describe other steps Emerson should take to report the change.

Exercise 21-3
Warranty expense

Key Services introduced a new line of lawn products in 2000 that carry a one-year warranty against manufacturer's defects. Because this was the first product for which the company offered a warranty, trade publications were consulted to determine the experience of others in the industry. Based on that experience, warranty costs were expected to approximate 3% of sales. Sales of the sprinklers in 2000 were $500,000. Accordingly, the following entries relating to the contingency for warranty costs were recorded during the first year of selling the product:

Accrued liability and expense		
Warranty expense (3% x $500,000)	15,000	
Estimated warranty liability		15,000
Actual expenditures (summary entry)		
Estimated warranty liability	4,600	
Cash, wages payable, parts and supplies, etc.		4,600

In late 2001, the company's claims experience was evaluated and it was determined that claims were far more than expected – 4% of sales rather than 3%.

Required:
1. Assuming sales of the sprinklers in 2001 were $720,000 and warranty expenditures in 2001 totaled $17,600, prepare any journal entries related to the warranty.
2. Assuming sales of the sprinklers were discontinued after 2000, prepare any journal entry(s) in 2001 related to the warranty.

PROBLEMS

Problem 21-1
Accounting changes; six situations

Described below are six independent and unrelated situations involving accounting changes. Each change occurs during 2000 before any adjusting entries or closing entries were prepared. Assume the tax rate for each company is 40% in all years. Any tax effects should be adjusted through the deferred tax liability account.

a. JB Industries introduced a new line of auto covers in 1999 that carry a one-year warranty against manufacturer's defects. Based on industry experience, warranty costs were expected to approximate 4% of sales. Sales of the covers in 1999 were $700,000. Accordingly, warranty expense and a warranty liability of $28,000 were recorded in 1999. In late 2000, the company's claims experience was evaluated and it was determined that claims were far fewer than expected: 3% of sales rather than 4%. Sales of the covers in 2000 were $800,000 and warranty expenditures in 2000 totaled $18,000

b. On December 30, 1996, Jefferson, Inc. acquired its office building at a cost of $4,000,000. It has been depreciated on a straight-line basis assuming a useful life of 40 years and no salvage value. However, plans were finalized in 2000 to relocate the company headquarters at the end of 2007. The vacated office building will have a salvage value at that time of $2,800,000.

c. Sterling Technology changed inventory cost methods to LIFO from FIFO at the end of 2000 for both financial statement and income tax purposes. Under FIFO, the inventory at January 1, 2001, is $13 million.

d. At the beginning of 1996, DD Corp. purchased office equipment at a cost of $990,000. Its useful life was estimated to be ten years with no salvage value. The equipment has been depreciated by the sum-of-the-years'-digits method. On January 1, 2000, the company changed to the straight-line method.

e. In October, 1998, the State of Florida filed suit against Master Industries, seeking penalties for violations of clean air laws. When the financial statements were issued in 1999, Master had not reached a settlement with state authorities, but legal counsel advises Master that it was probable the company would have to pay $40 million in penalties. Accordingly, the following entry was recorded:

Loss – litigation	40,000,000	
Liability - litigation..............................		40,000,000

Late in 2000, a settlement was reached with state authorities to pay a total of $45 million in penalties.

f. At the beginning of 2000, the Higher Tech, which uses the sum-of-the-years'-digits method changed to the straight-line method for newly acquired equipment. The change increased current year net earnings by $4.6 million.

Required:

For each situation:

- Identify the type of change.
- Prepare any journal entry necessary as a direct result of the change as well as any adjusting entry for 2000 related to the situation described.
- Briefly describe any other steps that should be taken to appropriately report the situation.

Problem 21-2
Correction of errors; six errors

Lawrence-Gabe Storage underwent a restructuring in 2000. The company conducted a thorough internal audit, during which the following facts were discovered. The audit occurred during 2000 before any adjusting entries or closing entries are prepared.

a. Additional printers were acquired at the beginning of 1998 and added to the company's office network. The $9,000 cost of the printers was inadvertently recorded as maintenance expense. The printers have five-year useful lives and no material salvage value. This class of equipment is depreciated by the straight-line method.

b. Three weeks prior to the audit, the company paid $51,000 for storage boxes and recorded the expenditure as office supplies. The error was discovered a week later.

c. On December 31, 1999, inventory was understated by $112,000 due to a mistake in the physical inventory count. The company uses the periodic inventory system.

d. Three years earlier, the company recorded a 3% stock dividend (4,000 common shares, $1 par) as follows:

Retained earnings	4,000	
Common stock		4,000

The shares had a market price at the time of $10 per share.

e. At the end of 1996, the company failed to accrue $60,000 of interest expense that accrued during the last four month's of 1999 on bonds payable. The bonds which were issued at face value mature in 2004. The following entry was recorded on March 1, 2000, when the semiannual interest was paid:

Interest expense	180,000	
Cash		180,000

f. A three-year liability insurance policy was purchased at the beginning of 1999 for $216,000. The full premium was debited to insurance expense at the time.

Required:
For each error, prepare any journal entry necessary to correct the error as well as any year-end adjusting entry for 2000 related to the situation described. (Ignore income taxes.)

EXERCISES

Exercise 22-1
Spreadsheet entries for cash paid to suppliers of merchandise

For each of the five independent situations below, prepare the spreadsheet entry that determines the amount of cash paid to suppliers and explains the change in each account shown. All dollars are in millions.

Situation	Cost of goods sold	Inventory increase (decrease)	Accounts payable increase (decrease)	Cash paid to suppliers
1	600	0	0	?
2	600	18	0	?
3	600	0	42	?
4	600	18	42	?
5	600	(18)	(42)	?

Exercise 22-2
Reconciliation of Net Cash Flows From Operating Activities to Net Income

The income statement and the "cash flows from operating activities" section of the statement of cash flows are provided below for Robert Mathis Company. The merchandise inventory account balance neither increased nor decreased during the reporting period. Mathis had no liability for either insurance, deferred income taxes, or interest at any time during the period.

Robert Mathis Company
INCOME STATEMENT
For the Year Ended December 31, 2000 ($ in millions)

Sales		$936
Cost of goods sold		(564)
Gross margin		$372
Salaries expense	$123	
Insurance expense	66	
Depreciation expense	33	
Depletion expense	15	
Bond interest expense	30	(267)
Gains and losses:		
Gain on sale of equipment		75
Loss on sale of land		(24)
Income before tax		$ 156
Income tax expense		(78)
Net Income		$ 78

Cash Flows From Operating Activities:

Cash received from customers	$774
Cash paid to suppliers	(525)
Cash paid to employees	(111)
Cash paid for interest	(27)
Cash paid for insurance	(48)
Cash paid for income taxes	(42)
Net cash flows from operating activities	$21

Required:
Prepare a schedule to reconcile Net Income to Net Cash Flows From Operating Activities.

Exercise 22-3
Cash Flows From Operating Activities (direct method) derived from an income statement and Cash Flows From Operating Activities (indirect method)

The income statement and a schedule reconciling "cash flows from operating activities" to net income are provided below ($ in 000) for Sun Technologies.

Sun Technologies
Income Statement
For The Year Ended
December 31, 2000

Sales		$915
Cost of goods sold		(555)
Gross margin		$360
Salaries expense	$123	
Insurance expense	57	
Depreciation expense	33	
Loss on sale of land	15	228
Income before tax		$132
Income tax expense		(66)
Net Income		$ 66

Reconciliation Of
Net Income To
Net Cash Flows
From Operating Activities

Net income	$66
***Adjustments for noncash effects*:**	
Depreciation expense	33
Loss on sale of land	15
Decrease in accounts receivable	18
Increase in inventory	(39)
Decrease in accounts payable	(24)
Increase in salaries payable	15
Decrease in prepaid insurance	27
Increase in income tax payable	60
Net cash flows from operating activities	$171

Required:

1. Calculate each of the following amounts for Sun Technologies:
   a. Cash received from customers during the reporting period.
   b. Cash paid to suppliers of goods during the reporting period.
   c. Cash paid to employees during the reporting period.
   d. Cash paid for insurance during the reporting period.
   e. Cash paid for income taxes during the reporting period.
2. Prepare the "Cash Flows From Operating Activities" section of the statement of cash flows (direct method).

Exercise 22-4
Indirect method: reconciliation of net income to net cash flows from operating

The accounting records of Close Company provided the data below:

Net loss	$25,000
Depreciation expense	30,000
Increase in salaries payable	2,500
Decrease in accounts receivable	10,000
Increase in inventory	11,500
Amortization of patent	1,500
Reduction in discount on bonds	1,000

Required:

Prepare a reconciliation of net income to net cash flows from operating activities.

PROBLEMS

Problem 22-1
Classifications of Cash Flows From Investing and Financing Activities

Listed below are transactions that might be reported as investing and/or financing activities on a statement of cash flows. Possible reporting classifications of those transactions are provided also.

Classifications

+ I	Investing activity (cash inflow)
– I	Investing activity (cash outflow
+ F	Financing activity (cash inflow)
– F	Financing activity (cash outflow)
N	Noncash investing and financing activity
X	Not reported as an investing and/or a financing activity

Transactions

Example +I 1. Sale of a building
______ 2. Issuance of preferred stock for cash
______ 3. Retirement of preferred stock
______ 4. Conversion of bonds to common stock
______ 5. Lease of a machine by capital lease
______ 6. Sale of a trademark
______ 7. Purchase of land for cash
______ 8. Issuance of common stock for a building
______ 9. Collection of a note receivable (principal amount)
______ 10. Sale of bonds payable
______ 11. Distribution of a stock dividend
______ 12. Payment of property dividend
______ 13. Payment of cash dividends
______ 14. Issuance of a short-term note payable for cash
______ 15. Issuance of a long-term note payable for cash
______ 16. Purchase of investment securities (not cash equivalent)
______ 17. Repayment of a note payable
______ 18. Cash payment for 3-year insurance policy
______ 19. Sale of land
______ 20. Issuance of note payable for land
______ 21. Purchase of common stock issued by another corporation
______ 22. Repayment of long-term debt by issuing common stock
______ 23. Restriction of retained earnings for plant expansion
______ 24. Payment of semiannual interest on notes payable
______ 25. Purchase of treasury stock
______ 26. Loan to a subsidiary
______ 27. Sale of merchandise to customers
______ 28. Purchase of treasury bills (cash equivalents)

Problem 22-2
Statement of cash flows: direct method; use spreadsheet

Comparative balance sheets for 2000 and 1999 and an income statement for 2000 are provided below for A2Z Industries. Additional information from the accounting records of A2Z also is provided.

A2Z Industries
Comparative Balance Sheets
December 31, 2000 and 1999 ($ in 000)

	2000	1999
Assets:		
Cash	$ 1,800	$ 1,125
Accounts receivable	1,800	1,350
Inventory	2,700	1,575
Land	2,025	1,800
Building	2,700	2,700
Less: Accumulated depreciation	(900)	(810)
Equipment	8,550	6,750
Less: Accumulated depreciation	(1,575)	(1,440)
Goodwill	3,600	4,500
	$20,700	$17,550
Liabilities:		
Accounts payable	$ 2,250	$ 1,350
Accrued expenses payable	900	675
Lease liability – land	450	0
Shareholders' Equity:		
Common stock	9,450	9,000
Paid-in capital - excess of par	2,250	2,025
Retained earnings	5,400	4,500
	$20,700	$17,550

A2Z Industries
Income Statement
For year ended December 31, 2000 ($ in 000)

Revenues:		
Sales revenue	$7,935	
Gain on sale of land	270	$8,205
Expenses:		
Cost of goods sold	$1,800	
Depreciation expense-building	90	
Depreciation expense-equipment	945	
Loss on sale of equipment	45	
Amortization of goodwill	900	
Operating expenses	1,500	5,280
Net income		$2,925

Additional information from the accounting records:

a. During 2000, equipment with a cost of $900,000 (90% depreciated) was sold.
b. The Statement of Shareholders' Equity reveals reductions of $675,000 and $1,350,000 for stock dividends and cash dividends, respectively.

Required:

Prepare the statement of cash flows of A2Z for the year ended December 31, 2000. Present "cash flows from operating activities" by the direct method and (unless your instructor directs you otherwise) use a spreadsheet to assist in your analysis. [You may omit the schedule to reconcile net income with cash flows from operating activities.]

Problem 22-4
Statement of cash flows; indirect method

Refer to the data provided in the previous problem for A2Z Industries.

Required:

Prepare the statement of cash flows for A2Z Industries using the *indirect method.*

Part II

Alternate Exercise and Problem Solutions

Chapter 1 Environment and Theoretical Structure of Financial Accounting

EXERCISES

Exercise 1-1

Requirement 1

Haskins and Price Operating Cash Flow		
	Year 1	**Year 2**
Cash collected	$330,000	$450,000
Cash disbursements:		
Payment of rent	(60,000)	- 0 -
Salaries	(200,000)	(210,000)
Travel	(50,000)	(60,000)
Utilities	(30,000)	(50,000
Net operating cash flow	$(10,000)	$130,000

Requirement 2

Haskins and Price Income Statements		
	Year 1	**Year 2**
Revenues	$380,000	$440,000
Expenses:		
Salaries	(200,000)	(210,000)
Utilities	(40,000)	(40,000)
Travel	(50,000)	(60,000)
Rent	(30,000)	(30,000)
Net Income	$ 60,000	$100,000

Requirement 3

Year 1:	Amounts billed to customers	$380,000
	Less: Cash collected	(330,000)
	Ending accounts receivable	$ 50,000

Year 2:	Beginning accounts receivable	$ 50,000
	Plus: Amounts billed to customers	440,000
		$490,000
	Less: Cash collected	(450,000)
	Ending accounts receivable	$ 40,000

Exercise 1-2

List A		List B
g	1. predictive value	a. applying the same accounting practices over time
h	2. relevance	b. record expenses in the period the related revenue is recognized
e	3. reliability	c. concerns the relative size of an item and its effect on decisions
j	4. comprehensive income	d. concerns the recognition of revenue
c	5. materiality	e. along with relevance, a primary decision-specific quality
a	6. consistency	f. the original transaction value upon acquisition
i	7. verifiability	g. information is useful in predicting the future
b	8. matching principle	h. pertinent to the decision at hand
f	9. historical cost principle	i. implies consensus among different measurers
d	10. realization principle	j. the change in equity from nonowner transactions

Exercise 1-3

1. The periodicity assumption
2. The matching principle
3. The historical cost or original transaction value principle
4. The full disclosure principle
5. The realization principle or revenue recognition principle
6. The economic entity assumption

Exercise 1-4

1. The periodicity assumption
2. The historical cost or original transaction value principle
3. The matching principle
4. The full disclosure principle
5. The economic entity assumption
6. The realization principle or revenue recognition principle

Chapter 2 Review of the Accounting Process

EXERCISES

Exercise 2-1

		Assets		=	Liabilities + Paid-in Capital + Retained Earnings		
1.	+	800,000	(cash)		+ 800,000 (capital stock)		
2.	-	15,000	(cash)				
	+	60,000	(equipment)		+ 45,000 (note payable)		
3.	+	270,000	(inventory)		+ 270,000 (accounts payable)		
4.	+	360,000	(accounts receivable)			+ 360,000	(revenue)
	-	210,000	(inventory)			- 210,000	(expense)
5.	-	20,000	(cash)			- 20,000	(expense)
6.	-	15,000	(cash)				
	+	15,000	(prepaid insurance)				
7.	-	180,000	(cash)		- 180,000 (accounts payable)		
8.	+	190,000	(cash)				
	-	190,000	(accounts receivable)				
9.	-	2,000	(accumulated depreciation)			- 2,000	(expense)

Exercise 2-2

	Account	Debit	Credit
1.	Cash	800,000	
	Capital stock		800,000
2.	Equipment	60,000	
	Note payable		45,000
	Cash		15,000
3.	Inventory	270,000	
	Accounts payable		270,000
4.	Accounts receivable	360,000	
	Sales revenue		360,000
	Cost of goods sold	210,000	
	Inventory		210,000
5.	Rent expense	20,000	
	Cash		20,000
6.	Prepaid insurance	15,000	
	Cash		15,000
7.	Accounts payable	180,000	
	Cash		180,000
8.	Cash	190,000	
	Accounts receivable		190,000
9.	Depreciation expense	2,000	
	Accumulated depreciation		2,000

Exercise 2-3

	Increase (I) or Decrease (D)	Account
1.	D	Accounts receivable
2.	D	Salary expense
3.	D	Loss on sale of land
4.	D	Prepaid insurance
5.	I	Interest revenue
6.	I	Capital stock
7.	I	Interest payable
8.	D	Land
9.	D	Interest expense
10.	I	Gain on sale of equipment
11.	D	Interest expense
12.	I	Accumulated depreciation
13.	D	Bad debt expense
14.	I	Sales revenue

Exercise 2-4

		Account(s) Debited	Account(s) Credited
Example:	Purchased equipment for cash	2	5
1.	Paid a cash dividend.	10	5
2.	Paid insurance for the next six months.	8	5
3.	Sold goods to customers on account.	4,16	9,3
4.	Purchased inventory for cash.	3	5
5.	Purchased supplies on account.	6	1
6.	Paid employees wages for November.	17	5
7.	Issued capital stock in exchange for cash.	5	12
8.	Collected cash from customers on account.	5	4
9.	Borrowed cash from a bank and signed a note.	5	11
10.	At the end of November, recorded the amount of supplies that had been used during the month.	7	6
11.	Paid October's interest on a bank loan.	13	5
12.	Accrued interest expense for November.	18	13

Exercise 2-5

1. Insurance expense (**$12,000 x 5/24**)	2,500	
Prepaid insurance		2,500
2. Depreciation expense	20,000	
Accumulated depreciation		20,000
3. Salaries expense	27,000	
Salaries payable		27,000
4. Interest receivable (**$50,000 x 8% x 3/12**)	1,000	
Interest revenue		1,000
5. Supplies	2,200	
Supplies expense		2,200

Exercise 2-6

Requirement 1

Supplies			
11/30 Balance	4,000	Expense	?
Purchased	6,000		
12/31 Balance	8,000		

Cost of supplies used = $4,000 + 6,000 - 8,000 = **$2,000**

Requirement 2

Prepaid rent			
11/30 Balance	10,000	Expense	?
12/31 Balance	7,000		

Rent expense for December = $10,000 – 7,000 = **$3,000**

Exercise 2-6 (concluded)

Requirement 3

Interest payable

		7,000	11/30 Balance
Interest paid	**?**	2,000	Accrued interest
		4,000	12/31 Balance

Cash paid during December = $7,000 + 2,000 – 4,000 = **$5,000**

Requirement 4

Unearned rent revenue

		4,500	11/30 Balance
Earned for Dec.	1,500		
		3,000	12/31 Balance

Rent revenue recognized each month = $6,000 x 1/4 = **$1,500**

December 31, 2000

Unearned rent revenue	1,500	
Rent revenue		1,500

PROBLEMS

Problem 2-1

Requirement 1

2000		Debit	Credit
July 1	Cash	1,000,000	
	Capital stock		1,000,000
July 2	Inventory	80,000	
	Accounts payable		80,000
July 4	Prepaid rent	10,000	
	Cash		10,000
July 10	Accounts receivable	120,000	
	Sales revenue		120,000
July 10	Cost of goods sold	75,000	
	Inventory		75,000
July 15	Cash	50,000	
	Note payable		50,000
July 20	Wages expense	15,000	
	Cash		15,000
July 24	Accounts payable	50,000	
	Cash		50,000
July 26	Cash	60,000	
	Accounts receivable		60,000
July 28	Utilities expense	1,500	
	Cash		1,500
July 31	Prepaid insurance	8,000	
	Cash		8,000

Problem 2-1 (continued)

Requirement 2

Cash

7/1 Bal.	0		
7/1	1,000,000	10,000	7/4
7/15	50,000	15,000	7/20
7/26	60,000	50,000	7/24
		1,500	7/28
		8,000	7/31
7/31 Bal.	1,025,500		

Accounts receivable

7/1 Bal.	0		
7/10	120,000	60,000	7/26
7/31 Bal.	60,000		

Inventory

7/1 Bal.	0		
7/2	80,000	75,000	7/10
7/31 Bal.	5,000		

Prepaid insurance

7/1 Bal.	0		
7/31	8,000		
7/31 Bal.	8,000		

Prepaid rent

7/1 Bal.	0		
7/4	10,000		
7/31 Bal.	10,000		

Accounts payable

		0	7/1 Bal.
7/24	50,000	80,000	7/2
		30,000	**7/31 Bal.**

Note payable

		0	7/1 Bal.
		50,000	7/15
		50,000	**7/31 Bal.**

Capital stock

		0	7/1 Bal.
		1,000,000	7/1
		1,000,000	**7/31 Bal.**

Problem 2-1 (concluded)

INCOME STATEMENT ACCOUNTS

Sales revenue

		0	7/1 Bal.
		120,000	7/10
		120,000	**7/31 Bal.**

Cost of goods sold

7/1 Bal.	0		
7/10	75,000		
7/31 Bal.	75,000		

Utilities expense

7/1 Bal.	0		
7/28	1,500		
7/31 Bal.	1,500		

Wages expense

7/1 Bal.	0		
7/20	15,000		
7/31 Bal.	15,000		

Requirement 3

Account Title	**Debits**	**Credits**
Cash	1,025,500	
Accounts receivable	60,000	
Inventory	5,000	
Prepaid rent	10,000	
Prepaid insurance	8,000	
Accounts payable		30,000
Note payable		50,000
Capital stock		1,000,000
Sales revenue		120,000
Cost of goods sold	75,000	
Wages expense	15,000	
Utilities expense	1,500	
Totals	1,200,000	1,200,000

Problem 2-2

		Debit	Credit
1.	Depreciation expense	22,000	
	Accumulated depreciation		22,000
2.	Wage expense **($7,000 – 5,000)**	2,000	
	Wages payable		2,000
3.	Interest expense **($50,000 x 8% x 9/12)**	3,000	
	Interest payable		3,000
4.	Supplies expense **($2,300 – 1,000)**	1,300	
	Supplies		1,300
5.	Unearned revenue	3,000	
	Sales revenue		3,000
6.	Rent expense	1,000	
	Prepaid rent		1,000

Chapter 3 The Income Statement and Statement of Cash Flows

EXERCISES

Exercise 3-1

Requirement 1

APEX COMPUTER CORPORATION
Income Statement
For the Year Ended December 31, 2000

Revenues and gains:		
Sales		$3,400,000
Interest revenue		35,000
Gain on sale of equipment		30,000
Total revenues and gains		3,465,000
Expenses and losses:		
Cost of goods sold	$2,250,000	
Administrative expense	450,000	
Selling expense	150,000	
Restructuring costs	400,000	
Interest expense	20,000	
Income tax expense *	78,000	
Total expenses and losses		3,348,000
Income before extraordinary item		117,000
Extraordinary item:		
Loss from hurricane damage **(net of $120,000 tax benefit)**		(180,000)
Net loss		$ (63,000)
Earnings per share:		
Income before extraordinary item		$ .23
Extraordinary item		(.36)
Net loss		$.(13)

* 40% x $195,000

Exercise 3-1 (concluded)

Requirement 2

APEX COMPUTER CORPORATION
Income Statement
For the Year Ended December 31, 2000

Sales revenue		$3,400,000
Cost of goods sold		2,250,000
Gross profit		1,150,000
Operating expenses:		
Administrative expense	$450,000	
Selling expense	150,000	
Restructuring costs	400,000	
Total operating expenses		1,000,000
Operating income		150,000
Other income (expense):		
Interest revenue	35,000	
Gain on sale of equipment	30,000	
Interest expense	(20,000)	
Total other income (expense), net		45,000
Income from continuing operations before income taxes		195,000
Income tax expense *		78,000
Income before extraordinary item		117,000
Extraordinary item:		
Loss from hurricane damage **(net of $120,000 tax benefit)**		(180,000)
Net loss		$ (63,000)
Earnings per share:		
Income before extraordinary item		$ .23
Extraordinary item		(.36)
Net loss		$.(13)

* 40% x $195,000

Exercise 3-2

BILIBONG COMPANY
Income Statement
For the Year Ended December 31, 2000

Income from continuing operations	$ 500,000
Discontinued operations:	
Loss from operations **(net of $100,000 tax benefit)**	(150,000)
Gain on disposal **(net of $96,000 tax expense) ***	144,000
Loss from discontinued operations	(6,000)
Net income	$ 494,000
Earnings per share:	
Income from continuing operations	$ 2.50
Loss from discontinued operations	(.03)
Net income	$ 2.47

*** Loss on disposal:**

Gain on sale of assets	$300,000
Operating loss, 6/1 - 12/3	(60,000)
Total before tax gain	240,000
Less: Income tax expense (40%)	(96,000)
Net of tax gain	$144,000

Exercise 3-3

Requirement 1

OTTOBONI CORPORATION
Income Statement
For the Year Ended December 31, 2000

Income from continuing operations	$600,000
Discontinued operations:	
Loss from operations **(net of $80,000 tax benefit)**	(120,000)
Loss on disposal **(net of $36,000 tax benefit) ***.....................	(54,000)
Loss from discontinued operations	(174,000)
Net income	$426,000

*** Estimated loss on disposal:**

Operating loss from 10-03-00 through 12-31-00	$ (70,000)
Estimated operating loss from 1-1-01 through estimated disposal date	(120,000)
Estimated gain on sale of assets ($2,200,000 - 2,100,000)	100,000
Net before-tax estimated loss on disposal	(90,000)
Income tax benefit (40%)	36,000
Net after-tax estimated loss on disposal	$ (54,000)

Exercise 3-3 (concluded)

Requirement 2

OTTOBONI CORPORATION
Income Statement
For the Year Ended December 31, 2000

Income from continuing operations	$600,000
Discontinued operations:	
Loss from operations **(net of $80,000 tax benefit)**	(120,000)
Gain (loss) on disposal *	- 0 -
Loss from discontinued operations	(120,000)
Net income	$480,000

*** Estimated Gain (Loss) on disposal:**

Operating loss from 10-03-00 through 12-31-00	$ (70,000)
Estimated operating loss from 1-1-01 through estimated disposal date	(120,000)
Estimated gain on sale of assets ($2,600,000 – 2,100,000)	500,000
Net before-tax estimated gain on disposal	$310,000

Since a gain is estimated and there is a realized operating loss from the measurement date to the end of the fiscal year, no gain or loss on disposal is reported in 2000. A disclosure note is required.

Exercise 3-4

Requirement 1

When an estimate is revised as new information comes to light, accounting for the change in estimate is quite straightforward. We do not restate prior years' financial statements to reflect the new estimate; nor do we report the cumulative effect of the change in current income. Instead, we merely incorporate the new estimate in any related accounting determinations from there on. If the after-tax income effect of the change in estimate is material, the effect on net income and earnings per share must be disclosed in a note, along with the justification for the change.

Requirement 2

	$2,500,000	Cost
$400,000		Old annual depreciation ([$2,500,000 – 100,000] ÷ 6 years)
x 1.5 years	600,000	Depreciation to date (1998-1999)
	1,900,000	Book value
	(200,000)	Less new salvage value
	1,700,000	Revised depreciable base
	÷ 8.5	Estimated remaining life (10 years – 1.5 years)
	$ 200,000	New annual depreciation

Exercise 3-5

1. d Purchase of equipment in exchange for a note payable.
2. a Payment of rent.
3. a Collection of cash from customers.
4. a Payment of interest on debt.
5. b Purchase of a bond of another company.
6. c Issuance of common stock for cash.
7. b Sale of land for cash.
8. a Receipt of interest on a note receivable.
9. b Receipt of principal on a note receivable.
10. c Payment of cash dividends to shareholders.
11. a Payment to suppliers of inventory.

PROBLEMS

Problem 3-1

AJAX COMPANY
Income Statement
For the Year Ended December 31, 2000

Sales revenue		$6,200,000
Cost of goods sold		3,500,000
Gross profit		2,700,000
Operating expenses:		
Administrative and selling	$1,500,000	
Restructuring costs	250,000	
Loss from landslide damage	75,000	
Total operating expenses		1,825,000
Operating income		875,000
Other income (expense):		
Interest revenue	100,000	
Interest expense	(150,000)	
Loss on sale of equipment	(40,000)	(90,000)
Income from continuing operations before income taxes		785,000
Income tax expense		314,000
Income from continuing operations		471,000
Extraordinary item:		
Gain on sale of land **(net of $800,000 tax benefit)**		1,200,000
Net income		$1,671,000

Note:

1. The restructuring costs are not an extraordinary item.
2. The loss caused by the landslide is not an extraordinary item.

Problem 3-2

Situation 1

Operating income from 8-6-00 through 12-31-00	$ 360,000
Estimated operating loss from 1-1-01 through estimated disposal date	(240,000)
Estimated gain on sale of assets	300,000
Net before-tax gain on disposal	$ 420,000

A $360,000 gain is recognized in 2000 - the amount of the realized operating income. The remaining $60,000 gain is recognized in 2001 if realized.

Situation 2

Operating loss from 8-6-00 through 12-31-00	$(120,000)
Estimated operating loss from 1-1-01 through estimated disposal date	(220,000)
Estimated loss on sale of assets	(330,000)
Net before-tax loss on disposal	$(670,000)

Recognize the total estimated loss of $670,000 in 2000, and only recognize a gain or loss in 2001 if there is a difference between the estimated and actual loss.

Situation 3

Operating income from 8-6-00 through 12-31-00	$ 120,000
Estimated operating income from 1-1-01 through estimated disposal date	240,000
Estimated loss on sale of assets	(500,000)
Net before-tax loss on disposal	$(140,000)

Recognize the total estimated loss of $140,000 in 2000, and only recognize a gain or loss in 2001 if there is a difference between the estimated and actual loss.

Situation 4

Operating income from 8-6-00 through 12-31-00	$ 500,000
Estimated operating loss from 1-1-01 through estimated disposal date	(150,000)
Estimated gain on sale of assets	300,000
Net before-tax gain on disposal	$ 650,000

A $500,000 gain is recognized in 2000 - the amount of the realized operating income. The remaining $150,000 gain is recognized in 2001 if realized.

Problem 3-2 (concluded)

Situation 5

Operating income from 8-6-00 through 12-31-00	$ 400,000
Estimated operating income from 1-1-01 through estimated disposal date	150,000
Estimated gain on sale of assets	300,000
Net before-tax gain on disposal	$ 850,000

A $400,000 gain is recognized in 2000 - the amount of the realized operating income. The remaining $450,000 gain is recognized in 2001 if realized.

Situation 6

Operating Loss from 8-6-00 through 12-31-00	$(120,000)
Estimated operating loss from 1-1-01 through estimated disposal date	(70,000)
Estimated gain on sale of assets	100,000
Net before-tax gain on disposal	$ (90,000)

All of the $90,000 estimated loss is recognized in 2000. A gain or loss is recognized in 2001 if there is a difference between the estimated and actual gain.

Situation 7

Operating loss from 8-6-00 through 12-31-00	$(300,000)
Estimated operating loss from 1-1-01 through estimated disposal date	(200,000)
Estimated gain on sale of assets	650,000
Net before-tax gain on disposal	$ 150,000

None of the $150,000 gain is recognized in 2000. The gain is recognized in 2001 if realized.

Chapter 4 Income Measurement and Profitability Analysis

EXERCISES

Exercise 4-1

Requirement 1

	2000	2001
Contract price	$2,600,000	$2,600,000
Actual costs to date	360,000	2,010,000
Estimated costs to complete	1,560,000	- 0 -
Total estimated costs	1,920,000	2,010,000
Estimated (actual) gross profit	$ 680,000	$ 590,000

Gross profit recognition:

2000: $$\frac{\$360{,}000}{\$1{,}920{,}000} = 18.75\% \times \$680{,}000 = \mathbf{\$127{,}500}$$

2001: $590,000 - 127,500 = **$462,500**

Requirement 2

2000	$ - 0 -
2001	$590,000

Requirement 3

Balance Sheet
At December 31, 2000

Current assets:

Accounts receivable		$ 110,000
Construction in progress	$487,500*	
Less: Billings	(430,000)	
Costs and profit in excess of billings		57,500

* Costs ($360,000) + profits ($127,500)

Exercise 4-1 (concluded)

Requirement 4

Balance Sheet At December 31, 2000	
Current assets:	
Accounts receivable	$ 110,000
Current liabilities:	
Billings **($430,000)** in excess of costs **($360,000)**	$ 70,000

Exercise 4-2

Requirement 1

	2000	**2001**	**2002**
Contract price	$12,000,000	$12,000,000	$12,000,000
Actual costs to date	3,000,000	7,000,000	12,800,000
Estimated costs to complete	6,000,000	5,600,000	- 0 -
Total estimated costs	9,000,000	12,600,000	12,800,000
Estimated gross profit (loss)	$ 3,000,000	$ (600,000)	$ (800,000)

Gross profit (loss) recognition:

2000: $\frac{\$3,000,000}{\$9,000,000}$ = 33.3333% x $3,000,000 = **$1,000,000**

2001: $(600,000) - 1,000,000 = **$(1,600,000)**

2002: $(800,000) - (600,000) = **$(200,000)**

Exercise 4-2 (continued)

Requirement 2

	2000		2001	
Construction in progress	3,000,000		4,000,000	
Various accounts		3,000,000		4,000,000
To record construction costs.				
Accounts receivable	3,800,000		3,500,000	
Billings on construction contract		3,800,000		3,500,000
To record progress billings.				
Cash	3,250,000		3,600,000	
Accounts receivable		3,250,000		3,600,000
To record cash collections.				
Construction in progress **(gross profit)**	1,000,000			
Cost of construction	3,000,000			
Revenue from long-term contracts **(33.3333% x $12,000,000)**		4,000,000		
To record gross profit.				
Cost of construction (2)			4,266,667	
Revenue from long-term contracts (1)				2,666,667
Construction in progress (loss)				1,600,000
To record expected loss.				

(1) and (2):

Percent complete = $7,000,000 ÷ $12,600,000 = 55.55%

Revenue recognized to date:	
55.55% x $12,000,000 =	$6,666,667
Less: Revenue recognized in 2000 (above)	(4,000,000)
Revenue recognized in 2001	2,666,667 (1)
Plus: Loss recognized in 2001 (above)	1,600,000
Cost of construction, 2001	$4,266,667 (2)

Exercise 4-2 (concluded)

Requirement 3

Balance Sheet		**2000**	**2001**
Current assets:			
Accounts receivable		$550,000	$450,000
Construction in progress	$4,000,000*		
Less: Billings	(3,800,000)		
Costs and profit in excess of billings		200,000	
Current liabilities:			
Billings **($7,300,000)** in excess of costs less loss **($6,400,000)**			$900,000

* Costs ($3,000,000) + profits ($1,000,000)

Exercise 4-3

Requirement 1

Year	Income recognized	
2000	$250,000	($400,000 - 150,000)
2001	- 0 -	
2002	- 0 -	
2003	- 0 -	
2004	- 0 -	
Total	$250,000	

Requirement 2

Year	Cash Collected	Cost Recovery(37.5%)	Gross Profit(62.5%)
2000	$100,000	$ 37,500	$ 62,500
2001	75,000	28,125	46,875
2002	75,000	28,125	46,875
2003	75,000	28,125	46,875
2004	75,000	28,125	46,875
Totals	$400,000	$150,000	$250,000

Requirement 3

Year	Cash Collected	Cost Recovery	Gross Profit
2000	$100,000	$100,000	- 0 -
2001	75,000	50,000	$ 25,000
2002	75,000	- 0 -	75,000
2003	75,000	- 0 -	75,000
2004	75,000	- 0 -	75,000
Totals	$400,000	$150,000	$250,000

Exercise 4-4

November 15, 2000	**To record franchise agreement and down payment**	
Cash **(50% x $25,000)**	12,500	
Note receivable	12,500	
Unearned franchise fee revenue		25,000

February 15, 2001	**To recognize franchise fee revenue**	
Unearned franchise fee revenue	25,000	
Franchise fee revenue		25,000

Exercise 4-5

Turnover ratios for Garret & Sons Music Company for 2000:

$$\text{Inventory turnover ratio} = \frac{\$6{,}000{,}000}{[\$850{,}000 + 700{,}000] \div 2}$$

$$= \underline{\underline{7.74 \text{ times}}}$$

$$\text{Receivables turnover ratio} = \frac{\$10{,}000{,}000}{[\$800{,}000 + 600{,}000] \div 2}$$

$$= \underline{\underline{14.29 \text{ times}}}$$

$$\text{Average collection period} = \frac{365}{14.29}$$

$$= \underline{\underline{25.5 \text{ days}}}$$

$$\text{Asset turnover ratio} = \frac{\$10{,}000{,}000}{[\$4{,}490{,}000 + 4{,}100{,}000] \div 2}$$

$$= \underline{\underline{2.33 \text{ times}}}$$

The company turns its inventory over 7 times per year compared to the industry average of 6 times per year. The asset turnover ratio also is slightly better than the industry average (2.33 times per year versus 2 times). These ratios indicate that Garret & Sons is able to generate more sales per dollar invested in inventory and in total assets than the industry averages. The company also is able to collect its receivables quicker than the industry average (25.5 days compared to the industry average of 28 days).

Exercise 4-6

Requirement 1

a. Profit margin on sales	\$360 ÷ \$7,200 = 5%
b. Return on assets	\$360 ÷ [(\$2,900 + 2,700) ÷ 2] = 12.86%
c. Return on shareholders' equity	\$360 ÷ [(\$1,700 + 1,550) ÷ 2] = 22.2%

Requirement 2

Retained earnings beginning of period	\$550,000
Add: Net income	360,000
	910,000
Less: Retained earnings end of period	700,000
Dividends paid	\$210,000

PROBLEMS

Problem 4-1

Requirement 1

	2000	2001	2002
Contract price	$15,000,000	$15,000,000	$15,000,000
Actual costs to date	4,000,000	8,800,000	13,000,000
Estimated costs to complete	8,000,000	4,000,000	- 0 -
Total estimated costs	12,000,000	12,800,000	13,000,000
Estimated gross profit (loss)	$ 3,000,000	$ 2,200,000	$ 2,000,000

Gross profit (loss) recognition:

2000: $\frac{\$4,000,000}{\$12,000,000}$ = 33.33% x $3,000,000 = **$1,000,000**

2001: $\frac{\$8,800,000}{\$12,800,000}$ = 68.75% x $2,200,000 = $1,512,500 - 1,000,000 = **$512,500**

2002: $2,000,000 - 1,512,500 = **$487,500**

Requirement 2

	2000		2001		2002	
Construction in progress	4,000,000		4,800,000		4,200,000	
Various accounts		4,000,000		4,800,000		4,200,000
To record construction costs.						
Accounts receivable	3,500,000		5,000,000		6,500,000	
Billings on construction contract		3,500,000		5,000,000		6,500,000
To record progress billings.						
Cash	2,800,000		5,600,000		6,600,000	
Accounts receivable		2,800,000		5,600,000		6,600,000
To record cash collections.						
Construction in progress **(gross profit)**	1,000,000		512,500		487,500	
Cost of construction **(cost incurred)**	4,000,000		4,800,000		4,200,000	
Revenue from long-term contracts(1)		5,000,000		5,312,500		4,687,500
To record gross profit.						

Problem 4-1 (continued)

(1) Revenue recognized:

2000: 33.33% x $15,000,000 =		$5,000,000
2001: 68.75% x $15,000,000 =	$10,312,500	
Less: Revenue recognized in 2000	(5,000,000)	
Revenue recognized in 2001		$5,312,500
2002: 100% x $15,000,000 =	$15,000,000	
Less: Revenue recognized in 2000 & 2001	(10,312,500)	
Revenue recognized in 2002		$4,687,500

Requirement 3

Balance Sheet		**2000**		**2001**
Current assets:				
Accounts receivable		$ 700,000		$100,000
Construction in progress	$5,000,000		$10,312,500	
Less: Billings	(3,500,000)		(8,500,000)	
Costs and profit in excess of billings		1,500,000		1,812,500

Requirement 4

	2000	**2001**	**1999**
Costs incurred during the year	$4,000,000	$4,200,000	$7,200,000
Estimated costs to complete as of year-end	8,000,000	7,100,000	-

	2000	**2001**	**1999**
Contract price	$15,000,000	$15,000,000	$15,000,000
Actual costs to date	4,000,000	8,200,000	15,400,000
Estimated costs to complete	8,000,000	7,100,000	- 0 -
Total estimated costs	12,000,000	15,300,000	15,400,000
Estimated gross profit (loss)	$ 3,000,000	$ (300,000)	$ (400,000)

Problem 4-1 (concluded)

Gross profit (loss) recognition:

2000: $\dfrac{\$4,000,000}{\$12,000,000}$ = 33.33% x \$3,000,000 = **\$1,000,000**

2001: 100% x \$(300,000) = \$(300,000) - 1,000,000 = **\$(1,300,000)**

2002: \$(400,000) – (300,000) = **\$(100,000)**

Problem 4-2

Requirement 1

Total profit = \$800,000 - 400,000 = \$400,000

Installment sales method: Gross profit % = \$400,000 ÷ \$800,000 = 50%

	10/31/00	**10/31/01**	**10/31/02**	**10/31/03**
Cash collections	\$200,000	\$200,000	\$200,000	\$200,000
a. Point of delivery method	\$400,000	- 0 -	- 0 -	- 0 -
b. Installment sales method (50% x cash collected)	\$100,000	\$100,000	\$100,000	\$100,000
c. Cost recovery method	- 0 -	- 0 -	\$200,000	\$200,000

Problem 4-2 (continued)

Requirement 2

	Point of Delivery		Installment Sales		Cost Recovery	
Installment receivable	800,000					
Sales revenue		800,000				
Cost of goods sold	400,000					
Inventory		400,000				
To record sale on 10/31/00.						
Installment receivable			800,000		800,000	
Inventory				400,000		400,000
Deferred gross profit				400,000		400,000
To record sale on 10/31/00.						
Cash	200,000		200,000		200,000	
Installment receivable		200,000		200,000		200,000
Entry made each Oct. 31.						
Deferred gross profit			100,000			
Realized gross profit				100,000		
To record gross profit.						
(entry made each Oct. 31)						
Deferred gross profit					200,000	
Realized gross profit						200,000
To record gross profit.						
(entry made 10/31/02 & 10/31/03)						

Problem 4-2 (concluded)

Requirement 3

	Point of Delivery	**Installment Sales**	**Cost Recovery**
December 31, 2000			
Assets			
Installment receivable	600,000	600,000	600,000
Liabilities			
Deferred gross profit from installment sale	- 0 -	300,000	400,000
December 31, 2001			
Assets			
Installment receivable	400,000	400,000	400,000
Liabilities			
Deferred gross profit from installment sale		200,000	400,000

Chapter 5 The Balance Sheet and Financial Disclosures

EXERCISES

Exercise 5-1

1.	b	Note receivable, due in 2 years	10.	a	Inventories
2.	a	Accounts receivable	11.	d	Goodwill
3.	-c	Accumulated depreciation	12.	f	Accrued salaries payable
4.	c	Land, in use	13.	f	Accrued taxes payable
5.	f	Note payable, due in 10 months	14.	a	Prepaid insurance
6.	f	Interest payable	15.	h	Common stock
7.	a	Note receivable, due in 6 months	16.	c	Equipment
8.	a	Cash equivalents	17.	f	Unearned revenue
9.	b	Investment in ABC Corp., long-term	18.	f	Warranties payable

Exercise 5-2

CURTIS CORPORATION Balance Sheet At December 31, 2000		
Assets		
Current assets:		
Cash and cash equivalents		$ 70,000
Marketable securities		15,000
Accounts receivable		110,000
Interest receivable		2,000
Inventories		120,000
Prepaid insurance		3,000
Total current assets		320,000
Investments and funds:		
Note receivable		50,000
Property, plant, and equipment:		
Machinery and equipment	$230,000	
Less: Accumulated depreciation	(111,000)	
Net property, plant, and equipment		119,000
Total assets		$489,000
Liabilities and Shareholders' Equity		
Current liabilities:		
Accounts payable		$ 45,000
Wages payable		10,000
Interest payable		3,000
Total current liabilities		58,000
Long-term liabilities:		
Bonds payable		100,000
Shareholders' equity:		
Common stock	$200,000	
Retained earnings	131,000	
Total shareholders' equity		331,000
Total liabilities and shareholders' equity		$489,000

Exercise 5-3

1. Depreciation method	A
2. Information on related party transactions	B
3. Method of accounting for acquisitions	A
4. Composition and details of long-term debt	B
5. Inventory method	A
6. Basis of revenue recognition	A
7. Major damage to a plant facility occurring after year-end	B
8. Composition of acrued liabilities	B

Exercise 5-4

1. Current ratio	[$150 + 400 + 500] ÷ $600 = 1.75
2. Acid-test ratio	[$150 + 400] ÷ $600 = .92
3. Debt to equity ratio	[$600 + 500] ÷ [$1,000 + 150] = .96
4. Times interest earned ratio	[$260 + 30 + 200] ÷ $30 = 16.3 times

Exercise 5-5

Action	Current Ratio	Acid-test Ratio	Debt to Equity Ratio
1. Issuance of common stock for cash	I	I	D
2. Purchase of inventory on account	I	D	I
3. Receipt of cash from a customer on account	N	N	N
4. Expiration of prepaid rent	D	N	I
5. Payment of a cash dividend	D	D	I
6. Purchase of equipment with a 6-month note	D	D	I
7. Purchase of long-term investment for cash	D	D	N
8. Sale of equipment for cash (no gain or loss)	I	I	N
9. Write-off of obsolete inventory	D	N	I
10. Decision to refinance on a long-term basis currently-maturing debt	I	I	N

PROBLEMS

Problem 5-1

ALEXANDRIA EXPLORATION CORPORATION
Balance Sheet
At December 31, 2000

Assets

Current assets:		
Cash and cash equivalents		$ 62,000
Short-term investments		130,000
Accounts receivable, net of allowance for uncollectible accounts of $15,000		155,000
Interest receivable		3,000
Inventories		200,000
Supplies		3,000
Total current assets		553,000
Investments:		
Land held for sale	$ 20,000	
Note receivable	50,000	
Total investments		70,000
Property, plant, and equipment:		
Land	80,000	
Buildings	500,000	
Machinery	250,000	
	830,000	
Less: Accumulated depreciation	(230,000)	
Net property, plant, and equipment		600,000
Intangibles:		
Goodwill		36,000
Total assets		$1,259,000

Liabilities and Shareholders' Equity

Current liabilities:		
Accounts payable		$ 125,000
Interest payable		40,000
Bonds payable		200,000
Total current liabilities		365,000
Long-term liabilities:		
Bonds payable		300,000
Shareholders' equity:		
Common stock, no par value; 1,000,000 shares authorized; 500,000 shares issued and outstanding	500,000	
Retained earnings	94,000	
Total shareholders' equity		594,000
Total liabilities and shareholders' equity		$1,259,000

Problem 5-2

TILLAMOO CHEESE COMPANY
Balance Sheet
At December 31, 2000

Assets

Current assets:		
Cash and cash equivalents		$ 190,000
Investment in stocks		40,000
Accounts receivable		300,000
Inventories		235,000
Prepaid expenses		15,000
Total current assets		780,000
Investments:		
Investment in bonds		260,000
Property, plant, and equipment:		
Land	$ 950,000	
Buildings	1,200,000	
Equipment	900,000	
	3,050,000	
Less: Accumulated depreciation	(600,000)	
Net property, plant, and equipment		2,450,000
Intangibles:		
Patent	80,000	
Goodwill	220,000	
Total intangibles		300,000
Total assets		$3,790,000

Liabilities and Shareholders' Equity

Current liabilities:		
Accounts payable		$ 260,000
Interest payable		20,000
Other accrued liabilities		60,000
Notes payable		180,000
Total current liabilities		520,000
Long-term liabilities:		
Notes payable	100,000	
Bonds payable	1,000,000	
Total long-term liabilities		1,100,000
Shareholders' equity:		
Common stock	1,500,000	
Retained earnings	670,000	
Total shareholders' equity		2,170,000
Total liabilities and shareholders' equity		$3,790,000

Chapter 6 Time Value of Money Concepts

EXERCISES

Exercise 6-1

1. FV = \$50,000 (2.15892*) = \$107,946

* Future value of \$1: n=10, i=8% (from Table 6A-1)

2. FV = \$30,000 (3.20714*) = \$96,214

* Future value of \$1: n=20, i=6% (from Table 6A-1)

3. FV = \$40,000 (17.44940*) = \$697,976

* Future value of \$1: n=30, i=10% (from Table 6A-1)

4. FV = \$60,000 (1.60103*) = \$96,062

* Future value of \$1: n=12, i=4% (from Table 6A-1)

Exercise 6-2

1. PV = \$20,000 (.46319*) = \$9,264

* Present value of \$1: n=10, i=8% (from Table 6A-2)

2. PV = \$10,000 (.31180*) = \$3,118

* Present value of \$1: n=20, i=6% (from Table 6A-2)

3. PV = \$25,000 (.05731*) = \$1,433

* Present value of \$1: n=30, i=10% (from Table 6A-2)

4. PV = \$40,000 (.40388*) = \$16,155

* Present value of \$1: n=8, i=12% (from Table 6A-2)

Exercise 6-3

1. PVA = $10,000 (3.79079*) = $37,908

* Present value of an ordinary annuity of $1: n=5, i=10% (from Table 6A-4)

2. PVAD = $10,000 (4.16986*) = $41,699

* Present value of an annuity due of $1: n=5, i=10% (from Table 6A-6)

Exercise 6-4

1. PV = $50,000 (.46319*) = $23,160

* Present value of $1: n=10, i=8% (from Table 6A-2)

2. $\frac{\$31,947}{\$70,000}$ = .45639*

* Present value of $1: n=20, i=**?** (from Table 6A-2, i = approximately **4%**)

3. $\frac{\$\ 9,576}{\$40,000}$ = .2394*

* Present value of $1: n=**?**, i=10% (from Table 6A-2, n = approximately **15 years**)

4. $\frac{\$\ 20,462}{\$100,000}$ = .20462*

* Present value of $1: n=14, i=**?** (from Table 6A-2, i = approximately **12%**)

5. FV = $15,000 (5.74349*) = $86,152

* Future value of $1: n=30, i=6% (from Table 6A-1)

Exercise 6-5

1. PVA = \$5,000 (6.14457*) = \$30,723

* Present value of an ordinary annuity of \$1: n=10, i=10% (from Table 6A-4)

2. $\frac{\$298,058}{\$60,000}$ = 4.96764*

* Present value of an ordinary annuity of \$1: n=8, i=**?** (from Table 6A-4, i = approximately **12%**)

3. $\frac{\$337,733}{\$30,000}$ = 11.25777*

* Present value of an ordinary annuity of \$1: n=**?**, i= 8% (from Table 6A-4, n = approximately **30 years**)

4. $\frac{\$600,000}{\$74,435}$ = 8.06072*

* Present value of an ordinary annuity of \$1: n=15, i=**?** (from Table 6A-4, i = approximately **9%**)

5. $\frac{\$200,000}{4.11141^*}$ = \$48,645

* Present value of an ordinary annuity of \$1: n=6, i=12% (from Table 6A-4)

Exercise 6-6

PV = ? x .80426* = \$4,800

PV = $\frac{\$4,800}{.80426^*}$ = \$5,968

* Present value of \$1: n=11, i=2% (from Table 6A-2)

PVA = ? (annuity amount) x 14.99203* = \$5,968

PVA = $\frac{\$5,968}{14.99203^*}$ = \$398.08 = Payment

* Present value of an ordinary annuity of \$1: n=18, i=2% (from Table 6A-4)

PROBLEMS

Problem 6-1

1. PV = \$50,000 + \$20,000 (3.31213*) = \$116,243 = Equipment

* Present value of an ordinary annuity of \$1: n=4, i=8% (from Table 6A-4)

2. \$600,000 = Annuity amount x 4.24646*

* Future value of an ordinary annuity of \$1: n=4, i=4% (from Table 6A-3)

$$\text{Annuity amount} = \frac{\$600{,}000}{4.24646}$$

Annuity amount = \$141,294 = Required annual deposit

3. Choose the option with the lowest present value of cash outflows.

1. *Buy option:*

PV = - \$2,000,000

2. *Lease option:*

PVAD = - \$200,000 (9.36492*) = - \$1,872,984

* Present value of an annuity due of \$1: n=10, i=10% (from Table 6A-6)

Reuter should **lease** the machine.

Problem 6-2

Choose the alternative with the highest present value.

Alternative 1:

PV = $400,000

Alternative 2:

PV = PVAD = $40,000 (10.29498*) = **$411,799**

* Present value of an annuity due of $1: n=15, i=6% (from Table 6A-6)

Alternative 3:

PVA = $45,000 x 9.71225* = $437,051

* Present value of an ordinary annuity of $1: n=15, i=6% (from Table 6A-4)

PV = $437,051 x .79209* = $346,184

* Present value of $1: n=4, i=6% (from Table 6A-2)

Smokey should choose alternative **2.**

Chapter 7 Cash and Receivables

EXERCISES

Exercise 7-1

Requirement 1

Step 1: Bank Balance to Corrected Balance

Balance per bank statement	$74,674
Add: Deposits outstanding	8,200
Deduct: Checks outstanding	(8,420)
Corrected cash balance	$74,454

Step 2: Book Balance to Corrected Balance

Balance per books	$78,984
Deduct:	
Service charges	(50)
NSF checks	(680)
Automatic monthly transfer	(2,000)
Error in recording cash disbursement ($2,000 – 200)	(1,800)
Corrected cash balance	$74,454

Requirement 2

To record credits to cash revealed by the bank reconciliation.

Miscellaneous expense **(bank service charges)**	50	
Accounts receivable **(NSF checks)**	680	
Cash - savings account	2,000	
Accounts payable	1,800	
Cash		4,530

Note: Each of the adjustments to the book balance required journal entries. None of the adjustments to the bank balance require entries.

Exercise 7-2

Requirement 1

Sales price = 200 units x $800 = $160,000 x 80% = *$128,000*

April 6, 2000		
Accounts receivable	128,000	
Sales revenue		128,000

April 16, 2000		
Cash **(99% x $128,000)**	126,720	
Sales discounts **(1% x $128,000)**	1,280	
Accounts receivable		128,000

Requirement 2

April 6, 2000		
Accounts receivable	128,000	
Sales revenue		128,000

May 6, 2000		
Cash	128,000	
Accounts receivable		128,000

Exercise 7-2 (concluded)

Requirement 3

Requirement 1:

April 6, 2000		
Accounts receivable	126,720	
Sales revenue **(99% x $128,000)**		126,720

April 16, 2000		
Cash	126,720	
Accounts receivable		126,720

Requirement 2:

April 6, 2000		
Accounts receivable	126,720	
Sales revenue **(99% x $128,000)**		126,720

May 6, 2000		
Cash	128,000	
Accounts receivable		126,720
Interest revenue		1,280

Exercise 7-3

Requirement 1

To record the write-off of receivables.

Allowance for uncollectible accounts	46,200	
Accounts receivable		46,200

Allowance for uncollectible accounts:	
Balance, beginning of year	$68,000
Deduct: Receivables written off	(46,200)
Balance, before adjusting entry for 2000 bad debts	21,800
Required allowance: 3% x $2,223,000	(66,690)
Bad debt expense	$44,890

To record bad debt expense for the year.

Bad debt expense	44,890	
Allowance for uncollectible accounts.........................		44,890

Requirement 2

Current assets:	
Accounts receivable, net of $66,690 in allowance for uncollectible accounts	$2,156,310

Exercise 7-4

Requirement 1

March 31, 2000		
Note receivable **(face amount)**	80,000	
Discount on note receivable **($80,000 x 6%)**		4,800
Sales revenue **(difference)**		75,200
December 31, 2000		
Discount on note receivable	3,600	
Interest revenue **($80,000 x 6% x $^9/_{12}$)**		3,600
March 31, 2001		
Discount on note receivable	1,200	
Interest revenue **($80,000 x 6% x $^3/_{12}$)**		1,200
Cash	80,000	
Note receivable **(face amount)**		80,000

Requirement 2

$ 4,800	interest for 12 months
÷ $75,200	sales price
= 6.38%	= effective interest rate

Exercise 7-5

Cash **(difference)**	99,000	
Loss on sale of receivables **(1% x $100,000)**	1,000	
Accounts receivable **(balance sold)**		100,000

Exercise 7-6

Requirement 1

Cash **(difference)**	99,000	
Loss on sale of receivables **(1% x $100,000)**....................	1,000	
Accounts receivable **(balance sold)**.............................		100,000

Requirement 2

Cash **(difference)**	99,000	
Discount on liability **(1% x $100,000)**	1,000	
Liability – financing arrangement		100,000
Accounts receivable factored..	100,000	
Accounts receivable		100,000

Exercise 7-7

Requirement 1

Step 1: Accrue interest earned.

September 1, 2000		
Interest receivable	1,000	
Interest revenue **($50,000 x 8% x $^3/_{12}$)**		1,000

Step 2: Add interest to maturity to calculate maturity value.
Step 3: Deduct discount to calculate cash proceeds.

$50,000	Face amount
4,000	Interest to maturity ($50,000 x 8%)
54,000	*Maturity value*
(4,050)	Discount ($54,000 x 10% x $^9/_{12}$)
$49,950	*Cash proceeds*

Step 4: To record a loss for the difference between the cash proceeds and the note's book value.

September 1, 2000		
Cash **(proceeds determined above)**	49,950	
Loss on sale of note receivable **(difference)**	1,050	
Note receivable **(face amount)**		50,000
Interest receivable **(accrued interest determined above)**		1,000

Requirement 2

Cash **(proceeds determined above)**	49,950	
Discount **(difference)**	1,050	
Liability – discounted note receivable **(face amount)**		51,000
Note receivable discounted	51,000	
Note receivable		50,000
Interest receivable		1,000

PROBLEMS

Problem 7-1

Requirement 1

Monthly bad debt expense accrual summary.

Bad debt expense **(2% x $3,800,000)**................................	76,000	
Allowance for uncollectible accounts.........................		76,000

To record year 2000 accounts receivable write-offs.

Allowance for uncollectible accounts	82,000	
Accounts receivable		82,000

Requirement 2

Bad debt expense	4,700	
Allowance for uncollectible accounts **(below)**............		4,700

Year-end required allowance for uncollectible accounts:

Summary

Age Group	**Amount**	**Percent Uncollectible**	**Estimated Allowance**
0-60 days	$ 825,000	2%	$ 16,500
61-90 days	220,000	10%	22,000
91-120 days	50,000	30%	15,000
Over 120 days	128,000	40%	51,200
Totals	$1,223,000		$104,700

Problem 7-1 (concluded)

Allowance for uncollectible accounts:

Beginning balance	$106,000
Add: Monthly bad debt accruals	76,000
Deduct: Write-offs	(82,000)
Balance before year-end adjustment	100,000
Required allowance (determined above)	104,700
Required year-end increase in allowance	$ 4,700

Requirement 3

Bad debt expense for 2000:

Monthly accruals	$76,000
Year-end adjustment	4,700
Total	$80,700

Balance sheet:

Current assets:	
Accounts receivable, net of $104,700 in allowance for uncollectible accounts	$1,118,300

Problem 7-2

Requirement 1

March 31, 2000		
Note receivable **(face amount)**	12,000	
Discount **($12,000 x 10%)**		1,200
Sales revenue **(difference)**		10,800

April 12, 2000		
Accounts receivable	10,000	
Sales revenue		10,000

April 21, 2000		
Cash **(98% x $10,000)**	9,800	
Sales discounts **(2% x $10,000)**	200	
Accounts receivable		10,000

April 27, 2000		
Sales returns	8,000	
Accounts receivable		8,000
Inventory	6,000	
Cost of goods sold		6,000

Problem 7-2 (continued)

May 30, 2000		
Cash **(98% x $100,000)**	98,000	
Loss on sale of receivables **(2% x $100,000)**	2,000	
Accounts receivable		100,000

July 31, 2000		
Note receivable	15,000	
Sales revenue		15,000

To accrue interest on note receivable for two months.

Sept. 30, 2000		
Interest receivable	200	
Interest revenue **($15,000 x 8% x 2/12)**		200

To record discounting of note receivable.

Sept. 30, 2000		
Cash **(proceeds determined below)**	14,976	
Loss on sale of note receivable **(difference)**	224	
Interest receivable **(from adjusting entry)**		200
Note receivable **(face amount)**		15,000

Problem 7-2 (concluded)

$15,000	Face amount
600	Interest to maturity ($15,000 x 8% x $^6/_{12}$)
15,600	*Maturity value*
(624)	Discount ($15,600 x 12% x $^4/_{12}$)
$14,976	*Cash proceeds*

Requirement 2

To accrue nine months' interest on the Misthos Co. note receivable.

Discount	900	
Interest revenue **($12,000 x 10% x $^9/_{12}$)**		900

Chapter 8 Inventories: Measurement

EXERCISES

Exercise 8-1

($ in 000s)

PERPETUAL SYSTEM			PERIODIC SYSTEM		
Purchases					
Inventory	265		Purchases	265	
Accounts payable		265	Accounts payable		265
Freight					
Inventory	16		Freight-in	16	
Accounts payable		16	Accounts payable		16
Returns					
Accounts payable	6		Accounts payable	6	
Inventory		6	Purchase returns		6
Sales					
Accounts receivable	350		Accounts receivable	350	
Sales revenue		350	Sales revenue		350
Cost of goods sold	264		No entry		
Inventory		264			
End of period					
No entry			Cost of goods sold (below)	264	
			Inventory (ending)	123	
			Purchase returns	6	
			Inventory (beginning)		112
			Purchases		265
			Freight-in		16

Cost of goods sold:

Beginning inventory		$112
Purchases	$265	
Less: Returns	(6)	
Plus: Freight-in	16	
Net purchases		275
Cost of goods available		387
Less: Ending inventory		(123)
Cost of goods sold		$264

Exercise 8-2

Requirement 1

Purchase price = 50 units x $800 = $40,000 x .75 = $30,000

January 14, 2000		
Purchases	30,000	
Accounts payable		30,000

January 23, 2000		
Accounts payable	30,000	
Purchase discounts **(2% x $30,000)**		600
Cash **(98% x $30,000)**		29,400

Requirement 2

January 14, 2000		
Purchases	30,000	
Accounts payable		30,000

February 13, 2000		
Accounts payable	30,000	
Cash		30,000

Exercise 8-2 (concluded)

Requirement 3

Requirement 1:

	Debit	Credit
January 14, 2000		
Purchases **(98% x $30,000)**	29,400	
Accounts payable		29,400

	Debit	Credit
January 23, 2000		
Accounts payable	29,400	
Cash		29,400

Requirement 2:

	Debit	Credit
January 14, 2000		
Purchases **(98% x $30,000)**	29,400	
Accounts payable		29,400

	Debit	Credit
February 13, 2000		
Accounts payable	29,400	
Interest expense **(2% x $30,000)**	600	
Cash		30,000

Exercise 8-3

Inventory balance before additional transactions	$317,000
Add:	
Materials purchased f.o.b. shipping point on 12/28	17,000
Deduct:	
Merchandise held on consignment from the Harvey Company	(12,000)
Correct inventory balance	$322,000

Exercise 8-4

First-in, first-out (FIFO)

Cost of goods sold:

Date of sale	Units sold	Cost of Units Sold	Total Cost
March 14	3,000 (from BI)	$8.00	$24,000
	1,000 (from 3/8 purchase)	8.40	8,400
March 25	4,000 (from 3/8 purchase)	8.40	33,600
	3,000 (from 3/18 purchase)	8.20	24,600
Total	11,000		$90,600

Ending inventory = 3,000 units x $8.20 = $24,600

Exercise 8-4 (continued)

Last-in, first-out (LIFO)

Date	Purchased		Sold		Balance	
Beginning inventory	3,000 @ $8.00 =	$24,000			3,000 @ $8.00	$24,000
March 8	5,000 @ $8.40 =	$42,000			3,000 @ $8.00 5,000 @ $8.40	$66,000
March 14			4,000 @ $ 8.40 =	$33,600	3,000 @ $8.00 1,000 @ $8.40	$32,400
March 18	6,000 @ $8.20 =	$49,200			3,000 @ $8.00 1,000 @ $8.40 6,000 @ $8.20	$81,600
March 25			6,000 @ $8.20 = 1,000 @ $8.40 =	$49,200 $ 8,400	3,000 @ $8.00	**$24,000** *Ending inventory*
	Total cost of goods sold		=	**$91,200**		

Exercise 8-4 (concluded)

Average cost

Date	Purchased		Sold		Balance	
Beginning inventory	3,000 @ \$8.00 =	\$24,000			3,000 @ \$8.00	\$24,000
March 8	5,000 @ \$8.40 =	\$42,000				
	\$66,000 / 8,000 units = \$8.25/unit					
March 14			4,000 @ \$8.25 =	\$33,000	4,000 @ \$8.25	\$33,000
March 18	6,000 @ \$8.20 =	\$49,200				
	\$82,200 / 10,000 units = \$8.22/unit					
March 25			7,000 @ \$8.22 =	\$57,540	3,000 @ \$8.22	**\$24,660** *Ending inventory*
	Total cost of goods sold		=	**\$90,540**		

Exercise 8-5

Requirement 1

Cost of goods available for sale:		
Beginning inventory (7,000 x $22.00)		$154,000
Purchases:		
6,000 x $22.65	$135,900	
9,000 x $24.00	216,000	351,900
Cost of goods available (22,000 units)		$505,900

Cost of goods available for sale (22,000 units)	$505,900
Less: Ending inventory (below)	(207,000)
Cost of goods sold	$298,900

Cost of ending inventory:

$$\text{Weighted-average unit cost} = \frac{\$505{,}900}{22{,}000 \text{ units}} = \$23 \text{ (rounded)}$$

9,000 units x $23 (rounded) = $207,000

Exercise 8-5 (concluded)

Requirement 2

Date	Purchased		Sold		Balance	
Beginning inventory	7,000 @ $22.00 =	$154,000			7,000 @ $22.00	$154,000
April 5	6,000 @ $22.65 =	$135,900				
	$289,900 / 13,000 units =	$22.30/unit				
April 11			5,000 @ $22.30 =	$111,500	8,000 @ $22.20	$178,400
April 26	9,000 @ $24.00 =	$216,000				
	$394,400 / 17,000 units =	$23.20/unit				
April 28			8,000 @ $23.20 =	<u>$185,600</u>	9,000 @ $23.20	**$208,800** *Ending inventory*
	Total cost of goods sold		=	**$297,100**		

Exercise 8-6

Date	Ending Inventory at Base Year Cost	Inventory Layers at Base Year Cost	Inventory Layers Converted to Cost	Ending Inventory DVL Cost
1/1/00	$832,000 / 1.00 = $832,000	$832,000 (base)	$832,000 x 1.00 = $832,000	$832,000
12/31/00	$954,000 / 1.02 = $935,294	$832,000 (base)	$832,000 x 1.00 = $832,000	
		103,294 (2000)	103,294 x 1.02 = 105,360	**937,360**
12/31/01	$975,000 / 1.05 = $928,571	$832,000 (base)	$832,000 x 1.00 = $832,000	
		96,571 (2000)	96,571 x 1.02 = 98,502	**930,502**

PROBLEMS

Problem 8-1

Requirement 1

Beginning inventory (8,000 x $10.00)		$ 80,000
Net purchases:		
Purchases (45,000* units x $12.00)	$540,000	
Less: Purchase discounts		
($11 x 40,000 units x 80% x 2%)	(7,040)	532,960
Cost of goods available (53,000 units)		612,960
Less: Ending inventory (below)		(70,000)
Cost of goods sold		$542,960

* The 5,000 units purchased on December 28 are included. The units were shipped f.o.b. shipping point before year-end. The $12 unit cost includes freight charges.

Cost of ending inventory:

Date of purchase	**Units**	**Unit cost**	**Total cost**
BI	7,000	$ 10.00	$ 70,000

Problem 8-2

Cost of goods available for sale for periodic system:

Beginning inventory (10,000 x $25.00)		$250,000
Purchases:		
8,000 x $24.00	$192,000	
7,000 x $27.00	189,000	381,000
Cost of goods available (25,000 units)		$631,000

1. FIFO, periodic system

Cost of goods available for sale (25,000 units)	$631,000
Less: Ending inventory (determined below)	(309,000)
Cost of goods sold	$322,000

Cost of ending inventory:

Date of purchase	Units	Unit cost	Total cost
Jan. 22	7,000	$27.00	$189,000
Jan. 4	5,000	24.00	120,000
Totals	12,000		$309,000

2. LIFO, periodic system

Cost of goods available for sale (25,000 units)	$631,000
Less: Ending inventory (determined below)	(298,000)
Cost of goods sold	$333,000

Cost of ending inventory:

Date of purchase	Units	Unit cost	Total cost
BI	10,000	$25.00	$250,000
Jan. 4	2,000	24.00	48,000
Totals	12,000		$298,000

Problem 8-2 (concluded)

3. Average cost, periodic system

Cost of goods available for sale (25,000 units)	$631,000
Less: Ending inventory (below)	(302,880)
Cost of goods sold	$328,120*

Cost of ending inventory:

$$\text{Weighted-average unit cost} = \frac{\$631{,}000}{25{,}000 \text{ units}} = \$25.24$$

12,000 units x $25.24 = $302,880

* Alternatively, could be determined by multiplying the units sold by the average cost: 13,000 units x $25.24 = $328,120

Chapter 9 Inventories: Additional Issues

EXERCISES

Exercise 9-1

Requirement 1

Product	(1) RC	(2) Ceiling NRV	(3) Floor NRV-NP (NP= 20% of cost)	(4) Designated Market Value [Middle value of (1)-(3)]	(5) Cost	Inventory Value [Lower of (4) or (5)]
Gloves	$330,000	$300,000	$228,000	$300,000	$360,000	$300,000
Bats	240,000	320,000	268,000	268,000	260,000	260,000
Balls	110,000	125,000	95,000	110,000	150,000	110,000
Uniforms	560,000	950,000	830,000	830,000	600,000	600,000
				Totals	$1,370,000	**$1,270,000**

The inventory value is **$1,270,000**.

Requirement 2

Loss from write-down of inventory: $1,370,000 – 1,270,000 = **$100,000**

Exercise 9-2

Merchandise inventory, January 1, 2000		$ 4,500,000
Purchases		14,500,000
Freight-in		1,000,000
Cost of goods available for sale		20,000,000
Less: Cost of goods sold:		
Sales	$23,000,000	
Less: Estimated gross profit of 40%	(9,200,000)	(13,800,000)
Estimated loss from fire		$ 6,200,000

Exercise 9-3

	Cost	Retail
Beginning inventory	$40,000	$60,000
Plus: Net purchases	28,250	37,000
Net markups		2,000
Less: Net markdowns		(1,500)
Goods available for sale	68,250	97,500

Cost-to-retail percentage: $\frac{\$68,250}{\$97,500} = 70\%$

	Cost	Retail
Less: Net sales		(45,000)
Estimated ending inventory at retail		$52,500
Estimated ending inventory at cost (70% x $52,500)	(36,750)	
Estimated cost of goods sold	$31,500	

Exercise 9-4

	Cost	Retail
Beginning inventory	$ 180,000	$ 300,000
Plus: Purchases	1,479,000	2,430,000
Freight-in	30,000	
Less: Purchase returns	(60,000)	(105,000)
Plus: Net markups		90,000
		2,715,000
Cost-to-retail percentage: $\frac{\$1,629,000}{\$2,715,000} = 60\%$		
Less: Net markdowns		(45,000)
Goods available for sale	1,629,000	2,670,000
Less:		
Normal spoilage		(63,000)
Net sales		(2,340,000)
Estimated ending inventory at retail		$ 267,000
Estimated ending inventory at cost (60% x $267,000)	(160,200)	
Estimated cost of goods sold	$1,468,800	

Exercise 9-5

	Cost	Retail
Beginning inventory	$213,840	$ 396,000
Plus: Net purchases	360,000	765,000
Net markups		18,000
Less: Net markdowns		(33,000)
Goods available for sale (excluding beginning inventory)	360,000	750,000
Goods available for sale (including beginning inventory)	573,840	1,146,000

Base year cost-to-retail percentage: $\frac{\$213,840}{\$396,000} = 54\%$

2000 cost-to-retail percentage: $\frac{\$360,000}{\$750,000} = 48\%$

	Cost	Retail
Less: Net sales		(690,000)
Estimated ending inventory at current year retail prices		$456,000
Estimated ending inventory at cost (below)	(238,838)	
Estimated cost of goods sold	$335,002	

Ending Inventory at Year-end Retail Prices	Step 1 Ending Inventory at Base Year Retail Prices	Step 2 Inventory Layers at Base Year Retail Prices	Step 3 Inventory Layers Converted to Cost	
$456,000 (above)	$\frac{\$456,000}{1.02} = \$447,059$	$396,000 (base)	x 1.00 x 54% =	$213,840
		51,059 (2000)	x 1.02 x 48% =	24,998

Total ending inventory at dollar-value LIFO retail cost **$238,838**

Exercise 9-6

1. To increase inventory by $1.6 million and increase retained earnings to what it would have been if 1999 cost of goods sold had been calculated correctly.

Analysis:

1999		2000	
Beginning inventory		Beginning inventory	U
Purchases		Purchases	
Less: Ending inventory	U		
Cost of goods sold	O		
Revenues			
Less: Cost of goods sold	O	U = Understated	
Less: Other expenses		O = Overstated	
Net income	U		
↓			
Retained earnings	U		

	($ in millions)	
Inventory	1.6	
Retained earnings		1.6

2. The 1999 financial statements that were incorrect as a result of the error would be *retroactively restated* to reflect the correct cost of goods sold, (income tax expense if taxes are considered), net income, ending inventory, and retained earnings when those statements are reported again for comparative purposes in the 2000 annual report.

3. Because retained earnings is one of the accounts incorrect, the correction to that account is reported as a *prior period adjustment* to the 1999 retained earnings balance in the comparative statements of shareholders' equity.

4. Also, a *disclosure note* should describe the nature of the error and the impact of its correction on each year's net income, income before extraordinary items, and earnings per share.

PROBLEMS

Problem 9-1

1. Average cost

		Cost	Retail
Beginning inventory		$140,000	$280,000
Plus: Purchases		420,000	690,000
Freight-in		16,000	
Less: Purchase returns		(12,000)	(18,000)
Plus: Net markups			24,000
Less: Net markdowns			(26,000)
Abnormal spoilage			(10,000)
Goods available for sale		564,000	940,000
Cost-to-retail percentage: $\frac{\$564,000}{\$940,000} = 60\%$			
Less:			
Normal spoilage			(5,000)
Sales:			
Net sales ($700,000 - 20,000)	$680,000		
Add back employee discounts	6,000		(686,000)
Estimated ending inventory at retail			$249,000
Estimated ending inventory at cost (60% x $249,000)		(149,400)	
Estimated cost of goods sold		$414,600	

Problem 9-1 (concluded)

2. Conventional (average, LCM)

		Cost	Retail
Beginning inventory		$140,000	$280,000
Plus: Purchases		420,000	690,000
Freight-in		16,000	
Less: Purchase returns		(12,000)	(18,000)
Plus: Net markups			24,000
Less: Abnormal spoilage			(10,000)
			966,000
Cost-to-retail percentage: $\frac{\$564,000}{\$966,000} = 58.39\%$			
Less: Net markdowns			(26,000)
Goods available for sale		564,000	940,000
Normal spoilage			(5,000)
Sales:			
Net sales ($700,000 - 20,000)	$680,000		
Add back employee discounts	6,000		(686,000)
Estimated ending inventory at retail			$249,000
Estimated ending inventory at cost (58.39% x $249,000)		(145,391)	
Estimated cost of goods sold		$418,609	

Problem 9-2

($ in 000s)

	Cost	Retail
Beginning inventory	$ 128	$ 200
Plus: Net purchases	1,072	1,600
Freight-in	59	
Net markups		6
Less: Purchase returns	(2)	(3)
Net markdowns		(13)
Goods available for sale (excluding beginning inventory)	1,129	1,590
Goods available for sale (including beginning inventory)	1,257	1,790

Base layer cost-to-retail percentage: $\frac{\$128}{\$200} = 64\%$

2000 layer cost-to-retail percentage: $\frac{\$1,129}{\$1,590} = 71\%$

	Cost	Retail
Less: Net sales		(1,465)
Estimated ending inventory at current year retail prices		$ 325
Estimated ending inventory at cost (calculated below)	(205)	
Estimated cost of goods sold	$1,052	

Ending Inventory at Year-end Retail Prices	Step 1 Ending Inventory at Base Year Retail Prices	Step 2 Inventory Layers at Base Year Retail Prices	Step 3 Inventory Layers Converted to Cost	
$325 (above)	$\frac{\$325}{1.08} = \$301$	$200 (base)	x 1.00 x 64% =	$128
		101 (2000)	x 1.08 x 71% =	77
Total ending inventory at dollar-value LIFO retail cost				$205

Chapter 10 Operational Assets: Acquisition

EXERCISES

Exercise 10-1

Calculation of goodwill:

Purchase price		$25,000,000
Less *fair* value of net assets:		
Book value of net assets	$16,250,000	
Plus: Fair value in excess of book value:		
Property, plant, and equipment	1,000,000	
Intangible assets	2,970,000	
Less: Book value in excess of fair value:		
Receivables	(150,000)	20,070,000
Goodwill		$ 4,930,000

Exercise 10-2

Requirement 1

Machine **($25,000 cash + $46,229 present value of note)**......	71,229	
Cash..		25,000
Note payable **(determined below)**		46,229

Present value of note payments:

PV = $10,000 (4.62288*) = $46,229

* Present value of an ordinary annuity of $1: n=6, i=8% (from Table 6A-4)

Requirement 2

Interest expense **($46,229 x 8%)**	3,698	
Note payable **(difference)**...	6,302	
Cash..		10,000

Requirement 3

Interest expense **[($46,229 - 6,302) x 8%]**	3,194	
Note payable **(difference)**...	6,806	
Cash..		10,000

Exercise 10-3

Truck - new **($800 + 14,000)**	14,800	
Accumulated depreciation **(balance)**	12,000	
Loss **($1,000 - 800)**	200	
Cash		14,000
Truck - old **(balance)**		13,000

This is an exchange of similar assets and no monetary consideration is received. The loss indicated (book value of old equipment less fair value) *is* recognized. The new equipment is valued at the fair value of the old equipment ($800) plus the cash given ($14,000).

Exercise 10-4

Truck - new **($1,000 + 14,000)**	15,000	
Accumulated depreciation **(balance)**	12,000	
Cash		14,000
Truck - old **(balance)**		13,000

This is an exchange of similar assets and no monetary consideration is received. The gain indicated of $500 (fair value of old equipment less book value) *is not* recognized. The new equipment is valued at the book value of the old equipment ($1,000) plus the cash given ($14,000).

Exercise 10-5

Research and development expense:

Salaries and wages for lab research	$ 350,000
Materials used in R&D projects	400,000
Equipment	85,000
Fees paid to outsiders for R&D projects	465,000
Total	$1,300,000

The patent filing and legal costs are capitalized as the cost of the patent. The in-process research and development costs are shown as a separate line item on the income statement, if material.

Exercise 10-6

Requirement 1

	($ in millions)	
Research and development expense	6	
Software development costs	4	
Cash		10

Requirement 2

(1) Percentage-of-revenue method:

$$\frac{\$5,000,000}{\$20,000,000} = 25\% \times \$4,000,000 = \$1,000,000$$

(2) Straight-line method:

1/3 or 33.33 % x $4,000,000 = $1,333,333

The straight-line method is used since it produces the greater amortization, **$1,333,333**.

Requirement 3

Software development costs	$4,000,000
Less: Amortization to date	(1,333,333)
Net	$2,666,667

PROBLEMS

Problem 10-1

Requirement 1

Brown:

Cash	40,000	
New asset **($125,000 - 40,000)**	85,000	
Accumulated depreciation - old asset **(balance)**	200,000	
Old asset **(balance)**		300,000
Gain on exchange of assets **(below)**		25,000

This is an exchange of dissimilar assets and a gain is indicated. The entire $25,000 indicated gain ($125,000 fair value of old asset - $100,000 book value) *is* recognized. The new asset is valued at the fair value of the old asset ($125,000) less the cash received ($40,000).

Filzinger:

New asset **($85,000 + 40,000)**	125,000	
Accumulated depreciation - old asset **(balance)**	220,000	
Cash		40,000
Old asset **(balance)**		278,000
Gain on exchange of assets **(below)**		27,000

This is an exchange of dissimilar assets and a gain is indicated. The gain of $27,000 ($85,000 fair value of old asset - $58,000 book value) *is* recognized. The new asset is valued at the market value of the old asset ($85,000) plus the cash given ($40,000).

Problem 10-1 (continued)

Requirement 2

Brown:

Cash	40,000	
New asset **(below)**	68,000	
Accumulated depreciation - old asset **(balance)**	200,000	
Old asset **(balance)**		300,000
Gain on exchange of assets **(below)**		8,000

This is an exchange of similar assets, a gain is indicated, and monetary consideration is received. A portion of the $25,000 indicated gain ($125,000 - $100,000) is recognized.

$$\frac{\text{Cash received}}{\text{Cash received + Fair value of similar asset received}}$$

$$\frac{\$40,000}{\$40,000 + \$85,000} = 32\%$$

Problem 10-1 (concluded)

Calculation of the Gain:

Determine Relative Fair Values of Assets Received:	**Fair Values**	**Relative Proportions**
Cash	$ 40,000	32%
New asset	85,000	68%
Total	$125,000	100%

Determine Portion of Old Asset Sold:	
Portion sold (32% x $100,000)	$ 32,000
Portion traded (68% x $100,000)	68,000
Total book value ($300,000 – 200,000)	$100,000

Determine Gain on Portion of Old Asset Sold:	
Cash received	$40,000
Portion sold (32% x $100,000)	(32,000)
Gain recognized on portion sold	$ 8,000

Filzinger:

New asset **($58,000 + 40,000)**	98,000	
Accumulated depreciation - old asset **(balance)**	220,000	
Cash		40,000
Old asset **(balance)**		278,000

This is an exchange of similar assets and a gain is indicated. The gain of $27,000 ($85,000 fair value of old asset - $58,000 book value) *is not* recognized. The new asset is valued at the book value of the old asset ($58,000) plus the cash given ($40,000).

Problem 10-2

Requirement 1

2000:

Expenditures for 2000:

Date	Amount		Fraction		Weighted
January 3, 2000	$500,000	x	12/12	=	$500,000
March 31, 2000	600,000	x	9/12	=	450,000
June 30, 2000	800,000	x	6/12	=	400,000
October 31, 2000	600,000	x	2/12	=	100,000
Accumulated expenditures (before interest) -	$2,500,000				
Average accumulated expenditures -					$1,450,000

Interest capitalized:

$1,450,000 x 10% = $145,000 = Interest capitalized

2001:

Date	Amount		Fraction		Weighted
January 1, 2001 ($2,500,000 + 145,000)	$2,645,000	x	6/6	=	$2,645,000
January 31, 2001	300,000	x	5/6	=	250,000
March 31, 2001	500,000	x	3/6	=	250,000
May 31, 2001	600,000	x	1/6	=	100,000
Accumulated expenditures (before interest) -	$4,045,000				
Average accumulated expenditures -					$3,245,000

Interest capitalized:

Amount		Rate		Fraction		Interest	
$2,000,000	x	10.0%	x	6/12	=	$100,000	
1,245,000	x	7.25%*	x	6/12	=	45,131	
$3,245,000						$145,131	= Interest capitalized

*** Weighted-average rate of all other debt:**

Debt		Rate		Interest
$5,000,000	x	8%	=	$400,000
3,000,000	x	6%	=	180,000
$8,000,000				$580,000

$$\frac{\$580,000}{\$8,000,000} = 7.25\%$$

Problem 10-2 (concluded)

Requirement 2

Accumulated expenditures 6/30/01, before interest capitalization (above)	$4,045,000
2001 interest capitalized (above)	145,131
Total cost of building	$4,190,131

Requirement 3

2000:

$2,000,000 x 10% =	$ 200,000
5,000,000 x 8% =	400,000
3,000,000 x 6% =	180,000
Total interest incurred	780,000
Less: Interest capitalized	(145,000)
2000 interest expense	$ 635,000

2001:

Total interest incurred	$ 780,000
Less: Interest capitalized	(145,131)
2001 interest expense	$ 634,869

Chapter 11 Operational Assets: Utilization and Disposition

EXERCISES

Exercise 11-1

1. Straight-line:

$$\frac{\$240{,}000 - 20{,}000}{8 \text{ years}} = \$27{,}500 \text{ per year}$$

2. Sum-of-the-years' digits:

Sum-of-the-digits is {[8 (8 + 1)]÷2} = 36

2000	\$220,000 x 8/36	=	\$48,889
2001	\$220,000 x 7/36	=	42,778

3. Double-declining balance:

Straight-line rate is 12.5% (1 ÷ 8 years) x 2 = 25% DDB rate

2000	\$240,000 x 25%	= \$60,000
2001	(\$240,000 - 60,000) x 25%	= \$45,000

4. One hundred fifty percent declining balance:

Straight-line rate is 12.5% (1 ÷ 8 years) x 1.5 = 18.75% rate

2000	\$240,000 x 18.75%	= \$45,000
2001	(\$240,000 – 45,000) x 18.75%	= \$36,563

5. Units-of-production:

$$\frac{\$240{,}000 - 20{,}000}{55{,}000 \text{ units}} = \$4 \text{ per unit depreciation rate}$$

2000	8,000 units x \$4	= \$32,000
2001	12,000 units x \$4	= \$48,000

Exercise 11-2

1. Straight-line:

$$\frac{\$240{,}000 - 20{,}000}{8 \text{ years}} = \$27{,}500 \text{ per year}$$

2000	$27,500 x 8/12	=	$18,333
2001	$27,500 x 12/12	=	$27,500

2. Sum-of-the-years' digits:

Sum-of-the-digits is {[8 (8 + 1)]/2} = 36

2000	$220,000 x 8/36 x 8/12	=	$32,593
2001	$220,000 x 8/36 x 4/12	=	$16,296
	+ $220,000 x 7/36 x 8/12	=	28,519
			$44,815

3. Double-declining balance:

Straight-line rate is 8% (1 ÷ 8 years) x 2 = 25% DDB rate

2000	$240,000 x 25% x 8/12	=	$40,000
2001	$240,000 x 25% x 4/12	=	$20,000
	+ ($240,000 – 60,000) x 25% x 8/12	=	30,000
			$50,000

or,

2001	($240,000 - 40,000) x 25%	=	$50,000

4. One hundred fifty percent declining balance:

Straight-line rate is 12.5% (1 ÷ 8 years) x 1.5 = 18.75% rate

2000	$240,000 x 18.75% x 8/12	=	$30,000
2001	$240,000 x 18.75% x 4/12	=	$15,000
	+ ($240,000 - 45,000) x 18.75% x 8/12	=	24,375
			$39,375

Or,

2001	($240,000 – 30,000) x 18.75%	=	$39,375

Exercise 11-2 (concluded)

5. Units-of-production:

$$\frac{\$220,000 - 20,000}{55,000 \text{ units}} = \$4 \text{ per unit depreciation rate}$$

2000	6,000 units x \$4 =	\$24,000
2001	12,000 units x \$4 =	\$48,000

Exercise 11-3

Requirement 1

$$\text{Depletion per ton} = \frac{\$2,000,000}{1,000,000 \text{ tons}} = \$2.00 \text{ per ton}$$

2000 depletion = \$2.00 x 400,000 tons = **\$800,000**

Requirement 2

Depletion is part of product cost and is included in the cost of the inventory of coal, just as the depreciation on manufacturing equipment is included in inventory cost. The depletion is then included in cost of goods sold in the income statement when the coal is sold.

Exercise 11-4

Requirement 1

a. To record the purchase of a patent.

June 30, 1998		
Patent	1,000,000	
Cash		1,000,000

To record amortization on the patent.

December 31, 1998		
Amortization expense **($1,000,000 ÷ 5 years x 1/2)**	100,000	
Patent		100,000
December 31, 1999		
Amortization expense **($1,000,000 ÷ 5 years)**	200,000	
Patent		200,000

b. To record the purchase of a franchise.

2000		
Franchise	40,000	
Cash		40,000

Exercise 11-4 (concluded)

Year-end adjusting entries

Patent: To record amortization on the patent.

December 31, 2000		
Amortization expense **(determined below)**	100,000	
Patent		100,000

Calculation of annual amortization after the estimate change:

($ in thousands)

$1,000	Cost
300	Amortization to date (1998-1999)
700	Unamortized cost (balance in the patent account)
÷ 7	Estimated remaining life
$100	New annual amortization

Franchise: To record amortization of franchise.

December 31, 2000		
Amortization expense **($40,000 ÷ 20 years)**........................	2,000	
Franchise		2,000

Requirement 2

Intangible assets:

Patent	$600,000	[1]
Franchise	38,000	[2]
Total intangibles	$638,000	

[1] $1,000,000 – 400,000
[2] $40,000 - 2,000

Exercise 11-5

Depreciation expense **(determined below)**	48,889	
Accumulated depreciation		48,889

Calculation of annual depreciation after the estimate change:

	$640,000	Cost
$60,000		Old annual depreciation ($600,000 ÷ 10 years)
x 3 years	180,000	Depreciation to date (1998-1999)
	460,000	Book value
	20,000	Revised residual value
	440,000	Revised depreciable base
	÷ 9	Estimated remaining life (12 years - 3 years)
	$ 48,889	New annual depreciation

Exercise 11-6

Analysis:

	Correct (Should Have Been Recorded)			Incorrect (As Recorded)	
1997	Machine	200,000		Expense 200,000	
	Cash		200,000	Cash	200,000
1997	Expense	22,500		Depreciation entry omitted	
	Accum. deprec.		22,500		
1998	Expense	22,500		Depreciation entry omitted	
	Accum. deprec.		22,500		
1999	Expense	22,500		Depreciation entry omitted	
	Accum. deprec.		22,500		

During the three-year period, depreciation expense was *understated* by \$67,500, but other expenses were *overstated* by \$200,000, so net income during the period was *understated* by \$132,500, which means retained earnings is currently *understated* by that amount.

During the three-year period, accumulated depreciation was understated, and continues to be understated by \$67,500.

To correct incorrect accounts

Machine	200,000	
Accumulated depreciation **(\$22,500 x 3 years)**...		67,500
Retained earnings **(\$200,000 – 67,500)**...............		132,500

PROBLEMS

Problem 11-1

1. Depreciation for 1998 and 1999.

December 31, 1998		
Depreciation expense **($60,000 ÷ 6 years x $^8/_{12}$)**	6,667	
Accumulated depreciation - equipment		6,667

December 31, 1999		
Depreciation expense **($60,000 ÷ 6 years)**.........................	10,000	
Accumulated depreciation - equipment		10,000

2. The year 2000 expenditure.

January 4, 2000		
Repair and maintenance expense	4,000	
Equipment..	11,000	
Cash..		15,000

3. Depreciation for the year 2000.

December 31, 2000		
Depreciation expense **(determined below)**........................	8,579	
Accumulated depreciation - equipment		8,579

Calculation of annual depreciation after the estimate change:

$ 60,000	Cost
16,667	Depreciation to date ($5,557 + 10,000)
43,333	Book value
11,000	Asset addition
54,333	New depreciable base
÷ 6 1/3	Estimated remaining life (8 years - 1 2/3 years)
$ 8,579	New annual depreciation

Problem 11-2

Requirement 1

Machine 651:

$$\frac{\$150{,}000 - 10{,}000}{10 \text{ years}} = \$14{,}000 \text{ per year } \times 3 \text{ years} = \quad \$42{,}000$$

Machine 652:

$$\frac{\$280{,}000}{7 \text{ years}} = \$40{,}000 \text{ per year } \times 2.5 \text{ years} = \quad 100{,}000$$

Machine 653:

$$\frac{\$110{,}000 - 5{,}000}{8 \text{ years}} = \$13{,}125 \text{ per year } \times 3/12 = \quad \underline{3{,}281}$$

Accumulated depreciation, 12/31/99 **$145,281**

Requirement 2

Building:

Useful life of the building:

$$\frac{\$300{,}000}{5 \text{ years}} = \$60{,}000 \text{ in depreciation per year}$$

(1995-1999)

$$\frac{\$1{,}250{,}000 - 50{,}000}{\$60{,}000} = 20\text{-year useful life}$$

Problem 11-2 (concluded)

To record depreciation on the building.

Depreciation expense **[($1,250,000 - 50,000) ÷ 20 years]**.....	60,000	
Accumulated depreciation - building..........................		60,000

To record depreciation on the equipment.

Depreciation expense **(determined below)**........................	74,725	
Accumulated depreciation - equipment......................		74,725

Equipment:

Machine 652 (determined above)		$40,000
Machine 653 (determined above)		13,125
Machine 651:		
Cost	$150,000	
Less: Accumulated depreciation	42,000	
Book value, 12/31/99	108,000	
Revised remaining life (8 years - 3 years)	÷ 5 years	21,600
		$74,725

Chapter 12 Investments

Exercise 12-1

Requirement 1

2000

March 1

	($ in millions)	
Investment in Platinum Gems, Inc. shares	124	
Cash		124

April 13

Investment in Oracle bonds	200	
Cash		200

July 20

Cash	3	
Investment revenue		3

October 13

Cash	10	
Investment revenue		10

October 14

Cash	205	
Investment in Oracle bonds		200
Gain on sale of investments		5

November 1

Investment in SPI preferred shares	40	
Cash		40

December 31

Adjusting entries:

Investment in Platinum Gems shares	4	
Unrealized holding gain on investments ([$64 x 2 million shares] - $124 million)		4

Exercise 12-1 (concluded)

	($ in millions)	
Unrealized holding loss on investments ([$74 x 500,000 shares] - $40 million)	3	
Investment in SPI preferred shares		3

2001

January 25

Cash ([2 million shares x $^1/_2$] x $65)	65	
Unrealized holding gain on investments ($^1/_2$ amount from adjusting entry)	2	
Gain on sale of investments (difference)		3
Investment in Platinum Gems shares ($128 million balance after adjusting entry x $^1/_2$)		64

March 1

Cash ($78 x 500,000 shares)	39	
Loss on sale of investments (difference)	1	
Unrealized holding loss on investments (from adjusting entry)		3
Investment in SPI preferred (balance after adjusting entry)		37

Requirement 2

2000 Income Statement

($ in millions)

Investment revenue (from July 20; Oct. 13) $13

Gain on sale of investments (from Oct. 14) 5

Note: Unlike for trading securities, unrealized holding gains and losses are not included in income for securities available for sale.

Exercise 12-2

1. Investments reported as current assets.

Security A	$ 725,000
Security B	200,000
Security C	560,000
Security E	980,000
Total	$2,465,000

2. Investments reported as noncurrent assets.

Security D	$ 865,000
Security F	409,000
	$1,274,000

3. Unrealized gain (or loss) component of income before taxes.

Trading Securities:

		Cost	*Fair value*	*Unrealized gain (loss)*
Security	A	$ 700,000	$ 725,000	$25,000
	B	210,000	200,000	(10,000)
Totals		$ 910,000	$ 925,000	$ 15,000

4. Unrealized gain (or loss) component of shareholders' equity.

Securities Available For Sale:

		Cost	*Fair value*	*Unrealized gain (loss)*
Security	C	$ 500,000	$ 560,000	$60,000
	D	850,000	865,000	15,000
Totals		$1,350,000	$1,425,000	$75,000

Exercise 12-3

	($ in millions)	
Purchase		
Investment in Reed's Restaurant Supplies shares..................	73	
Cash		73
Net income		
Investment in Reed's Rest. Supplies shares (35% x $20million)	7	
Investment revenue..		7
Dividends		
Cash (35% x 20 million shares x $1.10).......................................	7.7	
Investment in Reed's Restaurant Supplies shares...............		7.7
Adjusting entry		
No entry		

Exercise 12-4

	($ in millions)	
Purchase		
Investment in Conley Trucks	68	
Cash		68
Net income		
Investment in Conley Trucks shares (25% x $60 million)	15	
Investment revenue		15
Dividends		
Cash (5 million shares x $1.20)	6	
Investment in Conley Trucks shares		6
Depreciation		
Investment revenue ($10 million [calculation below‡] ÷ 5 years)	2	
Investment in Conley Trucks shares		2
Goodwill		
Investment revenue ($13 million [calculation below‡] ÷ 10 years)	1.3	
Investment in Conley Trucks shares		1.3

‡Calculations:

	Investee Net Assets ⇓	Net Assets Purchased ⇓	Difference Attributed to: ⇓
Cost		$76	
			Goodwill: $13
Fair value:	$252* x 25% =	$63	
			Undervaluation of assets: $10
Book value:	$212 x 25% =	$53	

*[$212 + 40] = $252

Adjusting entry

No entry

PROBLEMS

Problem 12-1

Requirement 1

		($ in 000s)
Purchase		
Investment in Austin shares	648	
Cash		648
Net income		
Investment in Austin shares (30% x $320,000)	96	
Investment revenue		96
Dividends		
Cash (20,000 shares x $3)	60	
Investment in Austin shares		60
Depreciation		
Investment revenue [calculation below‡] ÷ 8 years)	6	
Investment in Austin shares		6
Goodwill		
Investment revenue ($120,000 [calculation below‡] ÷ 10 years)	12	
Investment in Austin shares		12

‡**Calculations:**

	Investee Net Assets ⇓	Net Assets Purchased ⇓	Difference Attributed to: ⇓	
Cost		$648		
		}	*Goodwill:*	$120
Fair value:	$1,760* x 30%	=$528		
		}	*Undervaluation of assets:*	$48
Book value:	$1,600 x 30%	=$480		

*[$1,600 + 160] = $1,760

Adjusting entry

No entry

Problem 12-1 (concluded)

Requirement 2

Purchase	($ in 000s)	
Investment in Austin shares	648	
Cash		648
Net income		
No entry		
Dividends		
Cash (20,000 shares x $3)	60	
Investment revenue		60
Adjusting entry		
Unrealized holding loss on investments ([20,000 shares x $32] – $648,000)	8	
Investment in Austin shares		8

Problem 12-2

Requirement 1

	($ in millions)	
Purchase		
Investment in Monterrey shares	80.0	
Cash		80.0
Net income		
Investment in Monterrey shares (40% x $28 million)	11.2	
Investment revenue..		11.2
Dividends		
Cash (40% x $6 million)..	2.4	
Investment in Monterrey shares		2.4
Inventory		
Investment revenue ($1 million x 40%: all sold in 2000)	.4	
Investment in Monterrey shares		.4
Depreciation		
Investment revenue ([$4 million x 40%] ÷ 8 years)	.2	
Investment in Monterrey shares		.2
Goodwill		
Investment revenue ($16 million [calculation below‡] ÷ 10 years).........	1.6	
Investment in Monterrey shares		1.6

‡Calculations:

	Investee Net Assets ⇓	Net Assets Purchased ⇓	Difference Attributed to: ⇓	
Cost		$80		
			Goodwill:	$16 [plug]
Fair value:	$160* x 40% =	$64		
inventory	(1) x 40%		*Undervaluation of inventory:*	$0.4
plant facilities	(4) x 40%		*Undervaluation of plant:*	$1.6
Book value:	$155 x 40% =	$62		

* $155 +1 +4

Problem 12-2 (concluded)

Requirement 2

Investment Revenue

		($ in millions)
		11.2 Share of income
Inventory	.4	
Depreciation	.2	
Goodwill	1.6	
Balance		9.0

Requirement 3

Investment in Monterrey shares

		($ in millions)
Cost	80.0	
Share of income	11.2	
		2.4 Dividends
		.4 Inventory
		.2 Depreciation
		1.6 Goodwill
Balance	86.6	

Requirement 4

$80 million cash outflow from investing activities

$2.4 million cash inflow (dividends) among operating activities

Chapter 13 Current Liabilities

EXERCISES

Exercise 13-1

Requirement 1

Cash	6,000,000	
Notes payable		6,000,000

Requirement 2

Interest expense ($6,000,000 x 14% x $^4/_{12}$)	280,000	
Interest payable		280,000

Requirement 3

Interest expense ($6,000,000 x 14% x $^2/_{12}$)	140,000	
Interest payable (from adjusting entry)	280,000	
Notes payable (face amount)	6,000,000	
Cash (total)		6,420,000

Exercise 13-2

1.

Interest rate	Fiscal year-end
13%	December 31

$300 million x 13% x $^8/_{12}$ = $26 million

2.

Interest rate	Fiscal year-end
10%	October 31

$300 million x 10% x $^6/_{12}$ = $15 million

3.

Interest rate	Fiscal year-end
9%	June 30

$300 million x 9% x $^2/_{12}$ = $4.5 million

4.

Interest rate	Fiscal year-end
7%	January 31

$300 million x 7% x $^9/_{12}$ = $15.75 million

Exercise 13-3

2000

Jan. 22 No entry is made for a line of credit until a loan actually is made. It would be described in a disclosure note.

Mar. 1

Account	Debit	Credit
Cash	6,000,000	
Notes payable		6,000,000

June 1

Account	Debit	Credit
Interest expense ($6,000,000 x 10% x 3/12)	150,000	
Notes payable (face amount)	6,000,000	
Cash ($6,000,000 + 150,000)		6,150,000

Nov. 1

Account	Debit	Credit
Cash (difference)	5,640,000	
Discount on notes payable ($6,000,000 x 8% x 9/12)	360,000	
Notes payable (face amount)		6,000,000

Dec. 31

The effective interest rate is 8.5106% ($360,000 ÷ $5,640,000) x 12/9. So, properly, interest should be recorded at that rate times the outstanding balance times one-twelfth of a year:

Account	Debit	Credit
Interest expense ($5,640,000 x 8.5106% x 2/12)	80,000	
Discount on notes payable		80,000

However the same results are achieved if interest is recorded at the discount rate times the maturity amount times two-twelfths of a year:

Account	Debit	Credit
Interest expense ($6,000,000 x 8% x 2/12)	80,000	
Discount on notes payable		80,000

Exercise 13-3 (concluded)

2001

Aug. 1		
Interest expense ($6,000,000 x 8% x $^7/_{12}$)*	280,000	
Discount on notes payable		280,000
Notes payable (balance)	6,000,000	
Cash (maturity amount)		6,000,000

* or, ($5,640,000 x 8.5106% x $^7/_{12}$) = $280,000

Exercise 13-4

1. **Noncurrent liability: $22 million**
   The current liability classification includes (a) situations in which the creditor has the right to demand payment because an existing violation of a provision of the debt agreement makes it callable and (b) situations in which debt is not yet callable, but will be callable within the year if an existing violation is not corrected within a specified grace period – unless it's *probable* the violation will be corrected within the grace period. In this case, the existing violation is expected to be corrected within 6 months.

2. **Current liability: $9 million**
   The debt should be reported as a current liability because it is payable in the upcoming year, will not be refinanced with long-term obligations, and will not be paid with a bond sinking fund.

3. **Current liability: $15 million**
   The requirement to classify currently maturing debt as a current liability includes debt that is callable by the creditor in the upcoming year – even if the debt is not expected to be called

Exercise 13-5

Requirement 1

This is a loss contingency. There may be a future sacrifice of economic benefits (cost of satisfying the warranty) due to an existing circumstance (the warranted awnings have been sold) that depends on an uncertain future event (customer claims).

The liability is probable because product warranties inevitably entail costs. A reasonably accurate estimate of the total liability for a period is possible based on prior experience. So, the contingent liability for the warranty is accrued. The estimated warranty liability is credited and warranty expense is debited in 2000, the period in which the products under warranty are sold.

Requirement 2

2000 Sales		
Accounts receivable	7,500,000	
Sales		7,500,000
Accrued liability and expense		
Warranty expense (4% x \$7,500,000).....................	300,000	
Estimated warranty liability		300,000
Actual expenditures		
Estimated warranty liability	124,800	
Cash, wages payable, parts and supplies, etc. .		124,800

Requirement 3

Warranty Liability

	Debit	Credit	
		300,000	Estimated liability
Actual expenditures	124,800		
		175,200	Balance

PROBLEMS

Problem 13-1

Requirement 1

Blanton Plastics		
Cash	14,000,000	
Notes payable		14,000,000
N,C&I Bank		
Notes receivable	14,000,000	
Cash		14,000,000

Requirement 2

Adjusting entries (December 31, 2000)

Blanton Plastics		
Interest expense ($14,000,000 x 12% x $^{3}/_{12}$)	420,000	
Interest payable		420,000
N,C&I Bank		
Interest receivable	420,000	
Interest revenue ($14,000,000 x 12% x $^{3}/_{12}$)		420,000

Maturity (January 31, 2001)

Blanton Plastics		
Interest expense ($14,000,000 x 12% x $^{1}/_{12}$)	140,000	
Interest payable (from adjusting entry)	420,000	
Notes payable (face amount)	14,000,000	
Cash (total)		14,560,000
N,C&I Bank		
Cash (total)	14,560,000	
Interest revenue ($14,000,000 x 12% x $^{1}/_{12}$)		140,000
Interest receivable (from adjusting entry)		420,000
Notes receivable (face amount)		14,000,000

Problem 13-1 (concluded)

Requirement 3

Issuance of note (October 1, 2000)

Account	Debit	Credit
Cash (difference)..	13,440,000	
Discount on notes payable ($14,000,000 x 12% x 4/12)	560,000	
Notes payable (face amount)......................................		14,000,000

Adjusting entry (December 31, 2000)

Account	Debit	Credit
Interest expense ($14,000,000 x 12% x 3/12)...............	420,000	
Discount on notes payable..................................		420,000

Maturity (January 31, 2001)

Account	Debit	Credit
Interest expense ($14,000,000 x 12% x 1/12)...............	140,000	
Discount on notes payable..................................		140,000
Notes payable (face amount)......................................	14,000,000	
Cash		14,560,000

Effective interest rate:

Discount ($14,000,000 x 12% x 4/12)	$ 560,000
Cash proceeds	÷ $13,440,000
Interest rate for 4 months'	4.1666%
	x 12/4
Annual effective rate	12.5%

Problem 13-2

a. This is a loss contingency. Eastern can use the information occurring after the end of the year in determining appropriate disclosure. It is unlikely that Eastern would choose to accrue the $122 million loss because the judgment will be appealed and that outcome is uncertain. A disclosure note is appropriate:

Note X: Contingency
In a lawsuit resulting from a dispute with a supplier, a judgment was rendered against Eastern Corporation in the amount of $107 million plus interest, a total of $122 million at February 3, 2001. Eastern plans to appeal the judgment. While management and legal counsel are presently unable to predict the outcome or to estimate the amount of any liability the company may have with respect to this lawsuit, it is not expected that this matter will have a material adverse effect on the company.

b. This is a loss contingency. Eastern can use the information occurring after the end of the year in determining appropriate disclosure. Eastern should accrue the $140 million loss because the ultimate outcome appears settled and the loss is probable.

Loss – litigation..	140,000,000	
Liability - litigation		140,000,000

A disclosure note also is appropriate:

Notes: Litigation
In November 1999, the State of Nevada filed suit against the Company, seeking civil penalties and injunctive relief for violations of environmental laws regulating hazardous waste. On January 12, 2001, the Company announced that it had reached a settlement with state authorities on this matter. Based upon discussions with legal counsel, the Company, has accrued and charged to operations in 2000, $140 million to cover the anticipated cost of all violations. The Company believes that the ultimate settlement of this claim will not have a material adverse effect on the Company's financial position.

Problem 13-2 (concluded)

c. This is a gain contingency. Gain contingencies are not accrued even if the gain is probable and reasonably estimable. The gain should be recognized only when realized.

Though gain contingencies are not recorded in the accounts, they should be disclosed in notes to the financial statements.

> *Note X: Contingency*
> Eastern is the plaintiff in a pending lawsuit filed against United Steel for damages due to lost profits from rejected contracts and for unpaid receivables. The case is in final appeal. No amount has been accrued in the financial statements for possible collection of any claims in this litigation.

d. No disclosure is required because an IRS claim is as yet unasserted, and an assessment is not *probable*. Even if an unfavorable outcome is thought to be probable in the event of an assessment and the amount is estimable, disclosure is not required unless an unasserted claim is probable.

Problem 13-3

a. This is a loss contingency. Though a loss is probable, the amount of loss is not reasonably estimable. A disclosure note is appropriate:

> *Note X: Contingency*
> During 2000, the Company experienced labor disputes at three of its plants. The Company hopes an agreement will soon be reached. However negotiations between the Company and the unions have not produced an acceptable settlement and, as a result, strikes are ongoing at these facilities.

b. This is a gain contingency. Gain contingencies are not accrued even if the gain is probable and reasonably estimable. The gain should be recognized only when realized.

Though gain contingencies are not recorded in the accounts, they should be disclosed in notes to the financial statements.

> *Note X: Contingency*
> In accordance with a 1998 contractual agreement with A.J. Conner Company, the Company is entitled to $37 million for certain fees and expense reimbursements. The bankruptcy court has ordered A.J. Conner to pay the Company $23 million immediately upon consummation of a proposed merger with Garner Holding Group.

Problem 13-3 (concluded)

c. The contingency for warranties should be accrued:

Warranty expense ([2% x $2,100 million] – $1 million)	41,000,000	
Estimated warranty liability		41,000,000

The liability at December 31, 2000, is reported as $41 million:

Warranty Liability
(in millions)

Debit		Credit	
		39	Balance
Actual expenditures	39		
		41	Estimated liability
		41	Balance

d. This is a loss contingency. Even though the lawsuit occurred in 2001, the cause for the action occurred in 2000. Only a disclosure note is needed because an unfavorable outcome is reasonably possible, but not probable. Also, the amount is not reasonably estimable.

> *Note X: Contingency*
> Crump Holdings filed suit in January 2001 against the Company seeking $88 million, as an adjustment to the purchase price in connection with the Company's sale of its textile business in 2000. Crump alleges that the Company misstated the assets and liabilities used to calculate the purchase price for the division. The Company has answered the complaint and intends to vigorously defend the lawsuit. Management believes that the final resolution of the case will not have a material adverse effect on the Company's financial position.

Chapter 14 Bonds and Notes

EXERCISES

Exercise 14-1

Requirement 1

\$50 million	x	12%	x	2/12	=	\$1 million
face amount		annual rate		fraction of the annual period		accrued interest

Requirement 2

	($ in millions)	
Cash (\$47 million plus accrued interest)	48	
Discount on bonds (\$50 million – \$47 million)	3	
Bonds payable (face amount)		50
Interest payable (accrued interest determined above)		1

Exercise 14-2

1. Price of the bonds at January 1, 2000

Interest	$ 12,000,000¥	x	11.46992 *	=	$137,639,040
Principal	$240,000,000	x	0.31180 **	=	74,832,000
Present value (price) of the bonds					$212,471,040

¥ 5% x $240,000,000

* present value of an ordinary annuity of $1: n=20, i=6%

** present value of $1: n=20, i=6%

2. January 1, 2000

Cash (price determined above)	212,471,040	
Discount on bonds (difference)	27,528,960	
Bonds payable (face amount)		240,000,000

3. June 30, 2000

Interest expense (6% x $212,471,040)	12,748,262	
Discount on bonds payable (difference)		748,262
Cash (5% x $240,000,000)		12,000,000

4. December 31, 2000

Interest expense (6% x [$212,471,040 + 748,262)	12,793,158	
Discount on bonds payable (difference)		793,158
Cash (5% x $240,000,000)		12,000,000

Exercise 14-3

Requirement 1

Schmidt (Issuer)

Cash (102% x $60 million)..	61,200,000	
Convertible bonds payable (face amount)		60,000,000
Premium on bonds payable (difference).................		1,200,000

Facial Mapping (Investor)

Investment in convertible bonds (10% x $60 million)...	6,000,000	
Premium on bond investment (difference)	120,000	
Cash (102% x $6 million)..		6,120,000

Requirement 2

Schmidt (Issuer)

Interest expense ($2,700,000 - $60,000)	2,640,000	
Premium on bonds payable ($1,200,000 ÷ 20)............	60,000	
Cash (4.5% x $60,000,000)		2,700,000

Facial Mapping (Investor)

Cash (4.5% x $6,000,000)	270,000	
Premium on bond investment ($120,000 ÷ 20)		6,000
Interest revenue ($270,000 - $6,000)		264,000

[Using the straight-line method, each interest entry is the same.]

Requirement 3

Schmidt (Issuer)

Convertible bonds payable (10% of the account balance)	6,000,000	
Premium on bonds payable (($1,200,000 - [$60,000 x 11]) x 10%).....................	54,000	
Common stock ([6,000 x 40 shares] x $1 par)		240,000
Paid-in capital – excess of par (to balance)............		5,814,000

Facial Mapping (Investor)

Investment in common stock (to balance)....................	6,054,000	
Investment in convertible bonds (account balance)..		6,000,000
Premium on bond investment ($120,000 - [$600 x 11])		54,000

PROBLEMS

Problem 14-1

Requirement 1

	Cash Interest 4.5% x Face Amount	Effective Interest 5% x Outstanding Balance		Increase in Balance	Outstanding Balance
					193,537
1	9,000	.05(193,537) =	9,677	677	194,214
2	9,000	.05(194,214) =	9,711	711	194,925
3	9,000	.05(194,925) =	9,746	746	195,671
4	9,000	.05(195,671) =	9,784	784	196,455
5	9,000	.05(196,455) =	9,823	823	197,278
6	9,000	.05(197,278) =	9,864	864	198,142
7	9,000	.05(198,142) =	9,907	907	199,049
8	9,000	.05(199,049) =	9,951*	951	200,000
	72,000		**78,463**	**6,463**	

* rounded.

Requirement 2

	Cash Interest 4.5% x Face Amount	Recorded Interest Cash plus Discount Reduction		Increase in Balance $6,463 ÷ 8	Outstanding Balance
					193,537
1	9,000	(9,000 + 808) =	9,808	808	194,345
2	9,000	(9,000 + 808) =	9,808	808	195,153
3	9,000	(9,000 + 808) =	9,808	808	195,961
4	9,000	(9,000 + 808) =	9,808	808	196,769
5	9,000	(9,000 + 808) =	9,808	808	197,577
6	9,000	(9,000 + 808) =	9,808	808	198,385
7	9,000	(9,000 + 808) =	9,808	808	199,192*
8	9,000	(9,000 + 808) =	9,808	808	200,000
	72,000		**78,463**	**6,463**	

* rounded.

Problem 14-1 (continued)

Requirement 3

	Debit	Credit
(effective interest)		
Interest expense (5% x $196,455)	9,823	
Discount on bonds payable (difference)		823
Cash (4.5% x $200,000)		9,000
(straight-line)		
Interest expense (9,000 + 808)	9,808	
Discount on bonds payable (6,463 ÷ 8)		808
Cash (4.5% x $200,000)		9,000

Requirement 4

By the straight-line method, a company determines interest indirectly by allocating a discount or a premium *equally* to each period over the term to maturity. This is allowed if doing so produces results that are not materially different from the interest method. The decision should be guided by whether the straight-line method would tend to mislead investors and creditors in the particular circumstance.

Allocating the discount or premium equally over the life of the bonds by the straight-line method results in an **unchanging dollar amount** of interest each period. By the straight-line method, the amount of the discount to be reduced periodically is calculated, and the effective interest is the "plug" figure.

Unchanging dollar amounts like these are not produced when the effective interest approach is used. By that approach , the dollar amounts of interest vary over the term to maturity because the **percentage rate** of interest remains constant, but is applied to a changing debt balance.

Remember that the "straight-line method," is not an alternative method of determining interest in a conceptual sense, but is an application of the **materiality concept**. The appropriate application of GAAP, the effective interest method, is by-passed as a practical expediency in situations when doing so has no "material" effect on the results.

Problem 14-1 (concluded)

Requirement 5

The amortization schedule in requirement 1 gives us the answer – $19,728. The outstanding debt balance after the June 30, 2002, interest payment (line 5) is the present value at that time ($197,278) of the remaining payments. Since $20,000 face amount of the bonds is 10% of the entire issue, we take 10% of the table amount.

This can be confirmed by calculating the present value:

Interest	$ 900¥	x	2.72325 *	=	$2,451
Principal	$20,000	x	0.86384 **	=	17,276
Present value (price) of the bonds					$19,727 (rounded)

¥ 4.5% x $20,000

* present value of an ordinary annuity of $1: n=3, i=5%

** present value of $1: n=3, i=5%

Problem 14-2

Requirement 1

Interest	$ 25,000¥	x	3.16987 *	=	$ 79,247
Principal	$500,000	x	0.68301 **	=	341,505
Present value (price) of the note					$420,752

¥ 5% x $500,000

* present value of an ordinary annuity of $1: n=4, i=10%

** present value of $1: n=4, i=10%

Operational assets (price determined above)	420,752	
Discount on notes payable (difference)	79,248	
Notes payable (face amount)		500,000

Requirement 2

Dec.31	Cash Interest	Effective Interest		Increase in Balance	Outstanding Balance
					420,752
2000	25,000	.10(420,753) =	42,075	17,075	437,827
2001	25,000	.10(437,827) =	43,783	18,783	456,610
2002	25,000	.10(456,610) =	45,661	20,661	477,271
2003	25,000	.10(477,271) =	47,729*	22,729	500,000
	100,000		**179,248**	**79,248**	

* **rounded**

Requirement 3

Interest expense (market rate x outstanding balance)..........	45,661	
Discount on notes payable (difference)......................		20,661
Cash (stated rate x face amount)		25,000

Problem 14-2 (concluded)

Requirement 4

$420,753	÷	3.16987	=	$132,735
amount of loan		(from Table 6A-4) n=4, i=10%		installment payment

Requirement 5

Dec.31	Cash Payment	Effective Interest 10% x Outstanding Balance			Decrease in Balance Balance Reduction	Outstanding Balance
						420,753
2000	132,735	.10(420,753)	=	42,075	90,660	330,093
2001	132,735	.10(330,093)	=	33,009	99,726	230,367
2002	132,735	.10(230,367)	=	23,037	109,698	120,669
2003	132,735	.10(120,669)	=	12,066*	120,669	0
	530,940			**110,187**	**420,753**	

*** rounded**

Requirement 6

Interest expense (market rate x outstanding balance)...........	23,037	
Note payable (difference)...	109,698	
Cash (payment determined above)................................		132,735

Problem 14-3

Requirement 1

Bonds payable (face amount)	100,000,000	
Premium on bonds ($^{20}/_{40}$ x $30,000,000)	15,000,000	
Gain on early extinguishment* (to balance)		13,000,000
Cash ($100,000,000 x 102%)		102,000,000

*The gain is reported as an extraordinary item.

Requirement 2

Bonds payable (face amount)	50,000,000	
Premium on bonds ($^{10}/_{40}$ x $30,000,000)	7,500,000	
Gain on early extinguishment* (to balance)		5,000,000
Cash (given)		52,500,000

*The gain is reported as an extraordinary item.

Problem 14-4

Requirement 1

	($ in millions)	
Land	9	
Gain on disposal		9
Note payable	60	
Accrued interest payable	6	
Land		48
Gain on debt restructuring*		18

* The gain is reported as an extraordinary item.

Requirement 2

Analysis: *Carrying amount*: $60 million + $6 million = $66,000,000
Future payments: ($3 million x 4) + $45 million = 57,000,000
Loss to creditor / gain to debtor $ 9,000,000

	($ in millions)	
(a) January 1, 2000		
Accrued interest payable	6	
Note payable *	3	
Gain on debt restructuring**		9

* establishes a balance in the note account equal to the total cash payments under the new agreement ($60 million – 3 million = $57 million)

** The gain is reported as an extraordinary item.

(b) December 31, 2000, 2001, 2002, and 2003 revised "interest" payments		
Note payable	3	
Cash		3

Note: No interest expense should be recorded after the restructuring. All subsequent cash payments result in reductions of principal.

(c) December 31, 2003 revised principal payment		
Note payable	45	
Cash		45

Problem 14-4 (continued)

Requirement 3

Analysis:	*Carrying amount:*	$60,000,000 + $6,000,000 =	$66,000,000
	Future payments:		83,325,000
	Interest		$ 17,325,000

Calculation of the new effective interest rate:

- $66,000,000 ÷ $83,325,000 = .7921 – the Table 6A-2 value for n = 4, i = **?**
- In row 4 of Table 6A-2, the number .7921 is in the 6% column. So, this is the **new** effective interest rate.

(a) January 1, 2000

[Since the total future cash payments are not less than the carrying amount of the debt, no reduction of the existing debt is necessary and no entry is required at the time of the debt restructuring.]

Amortization Schedule (not required)

Dec.31	Cash Interest	Effective Interest 6% x Outstanding Balance	Increase in Balance	Outstanding Balance
				66,000,000
2000	0	.06 (66,000,000) = 3,960,000	3,960,000	69,960,000
2001	0	.06 (69,960,000) = 4,197,600	4,197,600	74,157,600
2002	0	.06 (74,157,600) = 4,449,456	4,449,456	78,607,056
2003	0	.06 (78,607,056) = 4,717,944*	4,717,944	83,325,000
	0	**17,325,000**	**17,325,000**	

* rounded

Problem 14-4 (concluded)

(b)

December 31, 2000		
Interest expense	3,960,000	
Interest payable		3,960,000
December 31, 2001		
Interest expense	4,197,600	
Interest payable		4,197,600
December 31, 2002		
Interest expense	4,449,456	
Interest payable		4,449,456
December 31, 2003		
Interest expense	4,717,944	
Interest payable		4,717,944
(c) December 31, 2003 revised payment		
Interest payable	23,325,000	
Note payable	60,000,000	
Cash		83,325,000

Chapter 15 Leases

EXERCISES

Exercise 15-1

(a) Gothic Corporation (Lessee)

June 30, 2000		
Rent expense.................................	40,000	
Cash		40,000
December 31, 2000		
Rent expense.................................	40,000	
Cash		40,000

(b) HardWhere (Lessor)

June 30, 2000		
Cash...	40,000	
Rent revenue..............................		40,000
December 31, 2000		
Cash...	40,000	
Rent revenue..............................		40,000
Depreciation expense ($350,000 ÷ 5 years)	70,000	
Accumulated depreciation..........		70,000

Exercise 15-2

Present Value of Minimum Lease Payments:

(\$10,000 x 10.78685*) = \$107,866

rental payments — present value

* present value of an annuity due of \$1: n=12, i=2%

[i = 2% (8% ÷ 4) because the lease calls for quarterly payments]

Lease Amortization Schedule

	Rental Payments	Effective Interest 2% x Outstanding Balance		Decrease in Balance	Outstanding Balance
					107,866
1	10,000			10,000	97,886
2	10,000	.02 (97,886) =	1,957	8,043	89,823
3	10,000	.02 (89,823) =	1,796	8,204	81,619
4	10,000	.02 (81,619) =	1,632	8,368	73,251
5	10,000	.02 (73,251) =	1,465	8,535	64,716
6	10,000	.02 (64,716) =	1,294	8,706	56,010
7	10,000	.02 (56,010) =	1,120	8,880	47,130
8	10,000	.02 (47,130) =	943	9,057	38,073
9	10,000	.02 (38,073) =	761	9,239	28,834
10	10,000	.02 (28,834) =	577	9,423	19,411
11	10,000	.02 (19,411) =	388	9,612	9,799
12	10,000	.02 (9,799) =	201*	9,799	0
	120,000		**12,134**	**107,866**	

* adjusted for rounding of other numbers in the schedule

Exercise 15-2 (concluded)

January 1, 2000		
Leased equipment (calculated above)	107,866	
Lease payable (calculated above)		107,866
Lease payable	10,000	
Cash (rental payment)		10,000
April 1, 2000		
Interest expense (2% x [$107,866 – 10,000])	1,957	
Lease payable (difference)	8,043	
Cash (rental payment)		10,000
July 1, 2000		
Interest expense (2% x $89,823: from schedule)	1,796	
Lease payable (difference)	8,204	
Cash (rental payment)		10,000
October 1, 2000		
Interest expense (2% x $81,619: from schedule)	1,632	
Lease payable (difference)	8368	
Cash (rental payment)		10,000
December 31, 2000		
Interest expense (2% x $73,251: from schedule)	1,465	
Interest payable		1,465
Depreciation expense ($107,866 ÷ 2 years)	53,933	
Accumulated depreciation		53,933
January 1, 2001		
Interest payable (from adjusting entry)	1,465	
Lease payable (difference)	8,535	
Cash (rental payment)		10,000

Exercise 15-3

Lease Amortization Schedule

	Rental Payments	Effective Interest 2% x Outstanding Balance		Decrease in Balance	Outstanding Balance
					107,866
1	10,000			10,000	97,886
2	10,000	.02 (97,886) =	1,957	8,043	89,823
3	10,000	.02 (89,823) =	1,796	8,204	81,619
4	10,000	.02 (81,619) =	1,632	8,368	73,251
5	10,000	.02 (73,251) =	1,465	8,535	64,716
6	10,000	.02 (64,716) =	1,294	8,706	56,010
7	10,000	.02 (56,010) =	1,120	8,880	47,130
8	10,000	.02 (47,130) =	943	9,057	38,073
9	10,000	.02 (38,073) =	761	9,239	28,834
10	10,000	.02 (28,834) =	577	9,423	19,411
11	10,000	.02 (19,411) =	388	9,612	9,799
12	10,000	.02 (9,799) =	201*	9,799	0
	120,000		**12,134**	**107,866**	

* adjusted for rounding of other numbers in the schedule

Exercise 15-3 (concluded)

	Debit	Credit
January 1, 2000		
Lease receivable ($10,000 x 12)	120,000	
Unearned interest revenue ($120,000 – 107,866)		12,134
Inventory of equipment (lessor's cost)		107,866
Cash (rental payment)	10,000	
Lease receivable		10,000
April 1, 2000		
Cash (rental payment)	10,000	
Lease receivable		10,000
Unearned interest revenue	1,957	
Interest revenue (2% x [$107866 – 10,000])		1,957
July 1, 2000		
Cash (rental payment)	10,000	
Lease receivable		10,000
Unearned interest revenue	1,796	
Interest revenue (2% x $89,826: from schedule)		1,796
October 1, 2000		
Cash (rental payment)	10,000	
Lease receivable		10,000
Unearned interest revenue	1,632	
Interest revenue (2% x $81,619: from schedule)		1,632
December 31, 2000		
Unearned interest revenue	1,465	
Interest revenue (2% x $73,251: from schedule)		1,465
January 1, 2001		
Cash (rental payment)	10,000	
Lease receivable		10,000

Exercise 15-4

Requirement 1

Lessor's Calculation of Rental Payments

Amount to be recovered (fair market value)		$107,866 ↓
Rent payments at the beginning of each of eight quarters:	↓ ($107,866 ÷ 10.7866**)	$10,000

** present value of an annuity due of $1: n=12, i=2%

Requirement 2

January 1, 2000

Lease receivable ($10,000 x 12)	120,000	
Cost of goods sold (lessor's cost)	90,000	
Sales revenue (fair market value)		107,866
Unearned interest revenue ($120,000 – 107,866)		12,134
Inventory of equipment (lessor's cost)		90,000
Cash (rental payment)	10,000	
Lease receivable		10,000

April 1, 2000

Cash (rental payment)	10,000	
Lease receivable		10,000
Unearned interest revenue	1,957	
Interest revenue (2% x [$107,866 – 10,000])		1,957

Exercise 15-5

Present value of periodic rental payments*

($205,542 x 7.49236**) $1,540,000

** present value of an annuity due of $1: n=13, i=11%

The lease meets at least one (actually 3 of 4 in this case) criteria for classification as a capital lease.

January 1, 2000

Cash (given)	1,540,000	
Helicopter (carrying value)		1,240,000
Deferred gain on sale-leaseback (difference)		300,000
Leased helicopter (present value of lease payments)	1,540,000	
Lease payable (present value of lease payments)		1,540,000
Lease payable	205,542	
Cash		205,542

December 31, 2000

Interest expense (11% x [$1,540,000 – 205,542])	146,790	
Interest payable		146,790
Depreciation expense ($1,540,000 ÷ 15 years*)	102,267	
Accumulated depreciation		102,267
Deferred gain on sale-leaseback ($300,000 ÷ 20 years)	15,000	
Depreciation expense		15,000

* The helicopter is depreciated over its remaining useful life rather than the lease term because title transfers to the lessee.

PROBLEMS

Problem 15-1

Requirement 1

Capital lease to lessee; Direct financing lease to lessor.

Since the present value of minimum lease payments (same for both the lessor and the lessee) is equal to (>90%) the fair value of the asset, the 90% recovery criterion is met.

Calculation of the Present Value of Minimum Lease Payments

Present value of periodic rental payments

$32,629 x 15.32380** = $500,000 (rounded)

** present value of an annuity due of $1: n=20, i=3%

The 75% of useful life criterion is met also. Both additional lessor conditions are met for a nonoperating lease. There is no dealer's profit because the fair value equals the lessor's cost.

Requirement 2

Pal Learning Systems (Lessee)
January 1, 2000

Leased equipment (calculated above)	500,000	
Lease payable (calculated above)		500,000
Lease payable	32,629	
Cash (rental payment)		32,629

April 1, 2000

Interest expense (3% x [$500,000 – 32,629])	14,021	
Lease payable (difference)	18,609	
Cash (rental payment)		32,629

Problem 15-1 (concluded)

Star Leasing (Lessor)
January 1, 2000

Lease receivable ($32,629 x 20)	652,580	
Unearned interest revenue ($652,580 - 500,000)		152,580
Inventory of equipment (lessor's cost)		500,000
Cash (rental payment)	32,629	
Lease receivable		32,629

April 1, 2000

Cash (rental payment)	32,629	
Lease receivable		32,629
Unearned interest revenue	14,021	
Interest revenue (3% x [$500,000 – 32,629])		14,021

Requirement 3

Star Leasing (Lessor)
January 1, 2000

Lease receivable ($32,629 x 20)	652,580	
Cost of goods sold (lessor's cost)	450,000	
Sales revenue (fair market value)		500,000
Unearned interest revenue ($652,580 - 500,000)		152,580
Inventory of equipment (lessor's cost)		450,000
Cash (rental payment)	32,629	
Lease receivable		32,629

April 1, 2000

Cash (rental payment)	32,629	
Lease receivable		32,629
Unearned interest revenue	14,021	
Interest revenue (3% x [$500,000 – 32,629])		14,021

Problem 15-2

Requirement 1

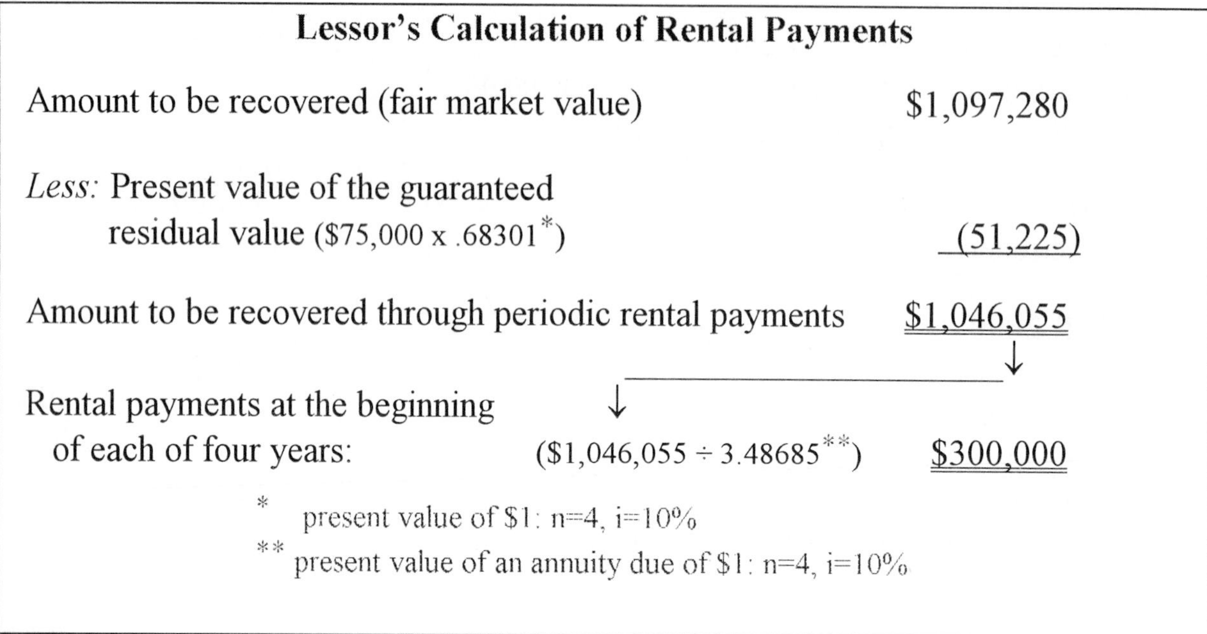

Lessor's Calculation of Rental Payments

Amount to be recovered (fair market value)		$1,097,280
Less: Present value of the guaranteed residual value ($75,000 x .68301*)		(51,225)
Amount to be recovered through periodic rental payments		$1,046,055
Rental payments at the beginning of each of four years:	($1,046,055 ÷ 3.48685**)	$300,000

* present value of $1: n=4, i=10%

** present value of an annuity due of $1: n=4, i=10%

Requirement 2

The lessee's incremental borrowing rate (12%) is more than the lessor's implicit rate (10%). So, both parties' calculations should be made using a 10% discount rate:

Problem 15-2 (continued)

Application of Classification Criteria

1 Does the agreement specify that ownership of the asset transfers to the lessee? — NO

2 Does the agreement contain a bargain purchase option? — NO

3 Is the lease term equal to 75% or more of the expected economic life of the asset? — NO {4 yrs < 75% of 6 yrs}

4 Is the present value of the minimum lease payments equal to or greater than 90% of the fair value of the asset? — YES {$1,046,055[b] > 90% of $1,046,055}

[b] See calculation below.

Present Value of Minimum Lease Payments

Present value of periodic rental payments ($300,000 x 3.48685**)	$1,046,055
Plus: Present value of the lessee-guaranteed residual value ($75,000 x .68301*)	51,225
Present value of minimum lease payments	$1,097,280

* present value of $1: n=4, i=10%

** present value of an annuity due of $1: n=4, i=10%

Chapter 16 Accounting for Income Taxes

EXERCISES

Exercise 16-1

Since taxable income is less than accounting income, a future taxable amount will occur when the temporary difference reverses. This means a deferred tax liability should be recorded to reflect the future tax consequences of the temporary difference.

	($ in millions)	
Income tax expense (to balance)	28.0	
Deferred tax liability ([$80 million – 50 million] x 35%)		10.5
Income tax payable ($50 million x 35%)		17.5

Exercise 16-2

Income tax expense (to balance)	249,000	
Deferred tax asset ($90,000 x 40%)	36,000	
Income tax payable (given)		285,000

Exercise 16-3

Requirement 1

	($ in millions)	
	Current Year 2000	**Future Deductible Amounts**
Temporary difference:		(280)
Taxable income	720	
Enacted tax rate	40%	40%
Tax payable currently	288	
Deferred tax asset		(112) ↓

Deferred tax asset:

Ending balance	$ 112
Less: beginning balance ($300 x 40%)	(120)
Change in balance	$(8)

Journal entries at the end of 2000

Income tax expense (to balance)	296	
Deferred tax asset (determined above)		8
Income tax payable (determined above)		288
Valuation allowance – deferred tax asset	40	
Income tax expense		40

Of course, these two entries can be combined.

Exercise 16-3 (concluded)

Requirement 2

		($ in millions)	
Income tax expense (to balance)		296	
	Deferred tax asset (determined above)		8
	Income tax payable (determined above)		288
Income tax expense		16	
	Valuation allowance – deferred tax asset ([$^1/_2$ x $112]– $40)		16

Of course, these two entries can be combined.

Exercise 16-4

Requirement 1

	Current Year 2000	($ in thousands) Future Taxable Amounts 2001	2002	2003	Future Taxable Amounts
Accounting income	900				
Non-temporary difference:					
Municipal bond interest	(160)				
Temporary difference:					
Depreciation	(40)	(8)	8	40	40
Taxable income	700				
Enacted tax rate	40%				40%
Tax payable currently	280				
Deferred tax liability					16 ↓

Deferred tax liability:

Ending balance	$16
Less: beginning balance	0
Change in balance	$16

Journal entry at the end of 2000

	Debit	Credit
Income tax expense (to balance)	296	
Deferred tax liability (determined above)		16
Income tax payable (determined above)		280

Requirement 2

	($ in thousands)
Pretax accounting income	$900
Income tax expense	(296)
Net income	$604

Exercise 16-5

Income Statement
For the fiscal year ended June 30, 2000

	($ in millions)
Revenues	$415
Cost of goods sold	(175)
Gross profit	$240
Operating expenses	(90)
Income from continuing operations before income taxes	$150
Income tax expense	(60)
Income before extraordinary item and cumulative effect of accounting change	$90
Extraordinary casualty loss, less applicable income taxes of $2	(3)
Cumulative effect of change in depreciation methods, less applicable income taxes of $16	(24)
Net income	$63

PROBLEMS

Problem 16-1

Requirement 1

($ in millions)

	Current Year 2000	Future Taxable Amounts 2001	2002	2003	Future Taxable Amounts [total]
Accounting income	68				
Temporary difference:					
Lot sales	(48)	16	20	12	48
Taxable income	20				
Enacted tax rate	40%				40%
Tax payable currently	8				
Deferred tax liability					19.2 ↓

Deferred tax liability:

Ending balance	$19.2
Less: beginning balance	(0.0)
Change in balance	$19.2

Journal entry at the end of 2000

Income tax expense (to balance)	27.2	
Deferred tax liability (determined above)		19.2
Income tax payable (determined above)		8.0

Problem 16-1 (concluded)

Requirement 2

($ in millions)

	Current Year 2001	Future Taxable Amounts 2002	2003	Future Taxable Amounts [total]
Accounting income	60			
Temporary difference:				
Lot sales	16	20	12	32
Taxable income	44			
Enacted tax rate	40%			35%
Tax payable currently	17.6			
Deferred tax liability				11.2 ↓

Deferred tax liability:

Ending balance	$11.2
Less: beginning balance	(19.2)
Change in balance	$(8.0)

Journal entry at the end of 2001

Income tax expense (to balance)	9.6	
Deferred tax liability (determined above)	8.0	
Income tax payable (determined above)		17.6

Requirement 3

The balance in the deferred tax liability account at the end of 2001 would have been $12.8 million if the new tax rate had not been enacted:

Future taxable amounts	$32 million
Previous tax rate	40%
Deferred tax liability	$12.8 million

The effect of the change is included in income tax expense, because income tax expense is less than it would have been if the rate had not changed.

Problem 16-2

Requirement 1

($ in 000s)

	Prior Years 1998	1999	Current Year 2000	Future Deductible Amounts [total]
Accounting loss			(540)	
Non-temporary difference:				
Fine paid			20	
Temporary differences:				
Loss contingency			40	(40)
Taxable loss			(480)	
Loss carryback	(300)	(120)	420	
Loss carryforward			60	(60)
			0	(100)
Enacted tax rate	40%	40%	40%	40%
Tax payable (refundable)	(120)	(48)	0	
Deferred tax asset				(40) ↓

Deferred tax asset:

Ending balance	$ 40
Less: beginning balance	(0)
Change in balance	$40

Journal entry at the end of 2000

Receivable – income tax refund ($120 + 48)	168	
Deferred tax asset (determined above)	40	
Income tax benefit (to balance)		208

Requirement 2

($ in 000s)

Operating loss before income taxes		$540
Less: Income tax benefit:		
Tax refund from loss carryback	$168	
Future tax benefits	40	208
Net operating loss		$ 332

Problem 16-2 (concluded)

Requirement 3

($ in 000s)	Current Year 2001	Future Deductible Amounts
Accounting income	240	
Temporary differences:		
Loss contingency	(40)	
Operating loss carryforward	(60)	
Taxable income	140	0
Enacted tax rate	40%	40%
Tax payable	56	
Deferred tax asset		0 ↓

Deferred tax asset:	
Ending balance	$ 0
Less: beginning balance	(40)
Change in balance	$(40)

Journal entry at the end of 2001

Income tax expense (to balance)	96	
Deferred tax asset (determined above)		40
Income tax payable (determined above)		56

Chapter 17 Pensions

EXERCISES

Exercise 17-1

Requirement 1

	($ in millions)
Service cost	$60
Interest cost	36
Actual return on the plan assets, $27 million Adjusted for $3 million gain on the plan assets	(24)
Pension expense	$72

Requirement 2

Pension expense (calculated above)	72	
Prepaid (accrued) pension cost (difference)		12
Cash (given)		60

Exercise 17-2

	($ in millions)
ABO	$(585)
Plan assets	520
Minimum liability	$ (60)
Less: prepaid pension cost – debit balance	30*
Additional liability needed	$ (90)

* Pension expense (given)	200	
Prepaid (accrued) pension cost (difference)		10
Cash (given)		190

Prepaid (accrued) pension cost:

Beginning of the year	$40
Reduction from entry above	10
End of year	$30

	($ in millions)	
Intangible pension asset	90*	
Additional liability (calculated above)		90**

* The entire $90 million can be added to the intangible asset because its balance will not exceed the unrecognized prior service cost ($150 million)

** Data indicates no previous balance in the "additional liability" account

This adjustment achieves the objective of providing for a minimum liability of $60 million:

Additional liability – credit balance	$(90)
Prepaid (accrued) pension cost – debit balance	30
Pension liability (reported as a single amount on the balance sheet)	$(60)

PROBLEMS

Problem 17-1

Requirement 1

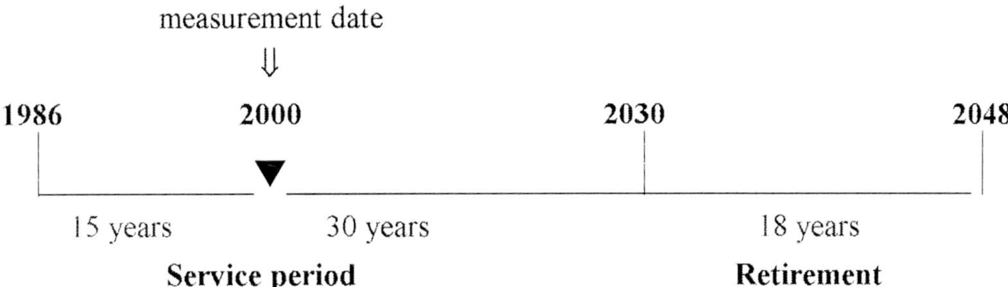

Requirement 2

1.5% x 15 x $80,000 = **$18,000**

Requirement 3

The present value of the retirement annuity as of the retirement date (end of 2030) is:

$18,000 x 10.05909* = **$190,636**

* present value of an ordinary annuity of $1: n=18, i=7%

The ABO is the present value of the retirement benefits at the end of 2000:

$190,636 x .13137* = **$25,044**

* present value of $1: n=30, i=7%

Requirement 4

1.5% x **18** x $85,000 = $22,950

$22,950 x 10.05909* = $230,856

$230,856 x .15040** = **$34,721**

* present value of an ordinary annuity of $1: n=18, i=7%

** present value of $1: **n=28**, i=7%

Problem 17-2

Requirement 1

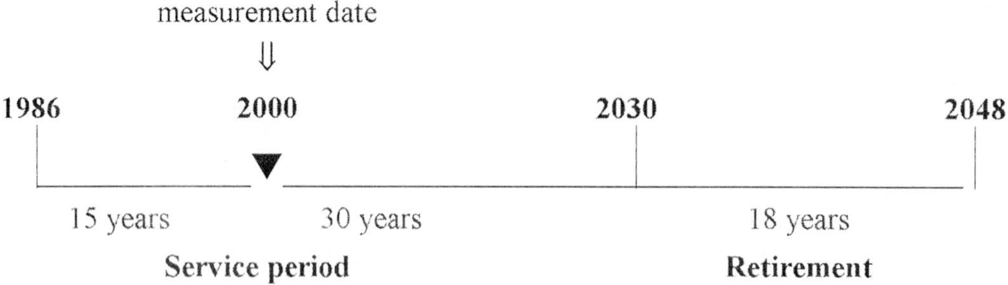

Requirement 2

1.5% x 15 x $250,000 = $56,250

Requirement 3

The present value of the retirement annuity as of the retirement date (end of 2030) is:

$56,250 x 10.05909* = $565,824

* present value of an ordinary annuity of $1: n=18, i=7%

The PBO is the present value of the retirement benefits at the end of 2000:

$565,824 x .13137* = $74,332

* present value of $1: n=30, i=7%

Requirement 4

1.5% x **18** x $250,000 = $67,500

$67,500 x 10.05909* = $678,989

$678,989 x .15040** = $102,120

* present value of an ordinary annuity of $1: n=18, i=7%

** present value of $1: **n=28**, i=7%

Problem 17-3

Requirement 1

1.5% x 14 x $250,000 = $52,500
$52,500 x 10.05909* = $528,102
$528,102 x .12277** = $64,835

* present value of an ordinary annuity of $1: n=18, i=7%
** present value of $1: n=31, i=7%

Requirement 2

1.5% x 1 x $250,000 = $3,750

Requirement 3

$3,750 x 10.05909* = $37,722
$37,722 x .13137** = $4,955

* present value of an ordinary annuity of $1: n=18, i=7%
** present value of $1: n=30, i=7%

Requirement 4

$64,835 x 7% = $4,538

Requirement 5

PBO at the *beginning* of 2000 (end of 1999)	$64,835
Service cost:	4,955
Interest cost: $64,835 x 7%	4,538
PBO at the *end* of 2000	$74,228

Note: In requirement 3 of the previous problem this same amount is calculated without separately determining the service cost and interest elements (allowing for a $4 rounding adjustment)

Problem 17-4

Requirement 1

PBO Without Amendment	PBO With Amendment
1.5% x 15 yrs x $250,000 = $56,250	**1.65%** x 15 yrs x $250,000 = $61,875
$56,250 x 10.05909* = $565,824	$61,875 x 10.05909* = $622,406
$565,824 x .13137** = $74,332 ↘	$622,406 x .13137** = $81,765 ↙

$7,434
Prior service cost

* present value of an ordinary annuity of $1: n=18, i=7%
** present value of $1: n=30, i=7%

Alternative calculation: 1.65 - 1.5 = **0.15%** x 15 yrs x $250,000 = $5,625
$5,625 10.05909* = $56,582
$56,582 x .13137** = $7,734

Requirement 2

$7,734 ÷ 20 years (expected remaining service) = $372

Requirement 3

1.65% x 1 x $250,000 = $4,125
$4,125 x 10.05909* = $41,494
$41,494 x .14056** = $5,832

* present value of an ordinary annuity of $1: n=18, i=7%
** present value of $1: **n=29**, i=7%

Requirement 4

$81,785 x 7% = $5,725

Requirement 5

Service cost (from req. 3)	$5,832
Interest cost (from req. 4)	5,725
Return on the plan assets (10% x $170,000)	(17,000)
Amortization of prior service cost (from req. 2)	372
Pension expense	$5,071

Problem 17-5

PBO With Previous Rate	PBO With Revised Rate
1.5% x 15 yrs x \$250,000 = \$56,250	1.5% x 15 yrs x \$250,000 = \$56,250
\$56,250 x 10.05909[1] = \$565,924	\$56,250 x 10.82763[3] = \$609,053
\$579,404 x .13137[2] = \$74,332 ↘	\$609,053 x .17411[4] = \$106,042 ↙

\$31,710
Loss on PBO

1 present value of an ordinary annuity of \$1: n=18, i=7%
2 present value of \$1: n=30, i=7%
3 present value of an ordinary annuity of \$1: n=18, i=6%
4 present value of \$1: n=30, i=6%

Chapter 18 Employee Benefit Plans

Exercise 18-1

	APBO	Service Cost
2000	$200,000 x 6/30 = $40,000	$200,000 x 1/30 = $6,667
2001	$216,000 x 7/30 = $50,400	$216,000 x 1/30 = $7,200

30 year attribution period (age 28-57)

Exercise 18-2

	($ in millions)	
Service cost	$61	
Interest cost	12	← (5% x [$210 + 30])
Return on plan assets	(0)	
Amortization of:		
transition obligation	5	←($100 ÷ 20 yrs)
prior service cost	2	←($30 ÷ 15 yrs)
Postretirement benefit expense	$80	

Exercise 18-3

Requirement 1

$25.50	fair value per share
x 12 million	shares granted
= $306 million	fair value of award

Requirement 2

no entry

Requirement 3

	($ in millions)	
Compensation expense ($306 million ÷ 3 years) ..	102	
Paid-in capital – restricted stock.................		102

Requirement 4

$25.50	fair value per share
x 12 million	shares granted
x 80%	100% – 20% forfeiture rate
= $244.8 million	fair value of award

Exercise 18-4

Requirement 1

At January 1, 2000, the estimated value of the award is:

$7	estimated fair value per option
x 75,000	options granted
= $525,000	total compensation

Requirement 2

Compensation expense ($525,000 ÷ 5 years)	105,000	
Paid-in capital – stock options		105,000

Requirement 3

Compensation expense (calculated below)	91,875	
Paid-in capital – stock options		91,875

At December 31, 2001, the estimated value of the award is:

$525,000	total compensation
x 90%	adjustment for 10% forfeiture
= $472,500	adjusted total compensation
- 105,000	expensed previously
$367,500	to be expensed
÷ 4 years	
= $91,875	expense in each of last four years

Exercise 18-5

Requirement 1

No liability or deferred compensation because the intrinsic value of the SARs is zero: [$23 – $23] x 48,000 shares = $0

Requirement 2

December 31, 2000	($ in 000s)	
Compensation expense*	32	
Liability – SAR plan....................................		32

* **Calculation:**

[$25-23] x 48,000	x	**1/3**	–	$0	=	**$32,000**
estimated total compensation		fraction of service to date		expensed earlier		current expense

December 31, 2001

No entry

* **Calculation:**

[$24-23] x 48,000	x	**2/3**	–	$32,000	=	**0**
estimated total compensation		fraction of service to date		expensed earlier		current expense

December 31, 2002		
Compensation expense*	64	
Liability – SAR plan....................................		64

* **Calculation:**

[$25-23] x 48,000	x	**3/3**	–	$32,000	=	**$64,000**
estimated total compensation		fraction of service to date		expensed earlier		current expense

Exercise 18-5 (concluded)

Requirement 3

Liability – SAR plan	48	
Compensation expense*		48

* **Calculation:**

[$24-23] x 48,000	x	all	–	[$32 + 64]	= $(48,000)
actual total compensation		fraction of service to date		expensed earlier	current expense

Liability – SAR plan (account balance)	48	
Cash...		48

Chapter 19 Shareholders' Equity

EXERCISES

Exercise 19-1

February 13

Cash (60 million shares x $10 per share)	600	
Common stock (60 million shares x $1 par)		60
Paid-in capital – excess of par (difference)		540

February 14

Legal expenses (1 million shares x $10 per share)	10	
Common stock (1 million shares x $1 par)		1
Paid-in capital – excess of par (difference)		9

Note: Because 60 million shares sold the previous day for $10 per share, it's reasonable to assume a $10 per share fair value.

February 14

Cash	90	
Common stock (3 million shares x $1 par)		3
Paid-in capital – excess of par, common*		27
Preferred stock (1 million shares x $50 par)		50
Paid-in capital – excess of par, preferred**		10

* 3 million shares x [$10 market value - $1 par].

** Since the value of the common shares is known ($30 million), the market value of the preferred ($60 million) is assumed from the total selling price ($90 million).

November 16

Property, plant, and equipment (cash value)	1,844,000	
Common stock (190,000 shares at $1 par per share)		190,000
Paid-in capital – excess of par (difference)		1,654,000

Exercise 19-2

1. January 8, 2000

	($ in millions)	
Common stock (8 million shares x $1 par)	8	
Paid-in capital – excess of par (8 million shares x $3*)	24	
Retained earnings (difference)	16	
Cash (8 million shares x $6 per share)		48

* Paid-in capital – excess of par: $1,200 ÷ 400 million shares

2. August 24, 2000

Common stock (16 million shares x $1 par)	16	
Paid-in capital – excess of par (16 million shares x $3)	48	
Paid-in capital – reacquired shares (difference)		24
Cash (16 million shares x $5.50 per share)		88

3. July 26, 2001

Cash (12 million shares x $7 per share)	84	
Common stock (12 million shares x $1 par)		12
Paid-in capital – excess of par (difference)		72

Exercise 19-3

Requirement 1

a. February 20 – declaration date

Investment in Brown International stock	15,000	
Gain on appreciation of investment ($500,000 - $485,000)		15,000
Retained earnings (100,000 shares at $5 per share)	500,000	
Property dividends payable		500,000

February 28 – date of record

no entry

March 20 – payment date

Property dividends payable	500,000	
Investment in Brown International stock		500,000

b. April 4

Paid-in capital – excess of par, common*	180,000	
Common stock (25% x [728,000 - 8,000] shares at $1 par) ...		180,000

**alternatively, retained earnings may be debited.*

c. July 25

Retained earnings (27,000* x $12 per share)	324,000	
Common stock (27,000* x $1 par)		27,000
Paid-in capital – excess of par, common (difference).......		297,000

* 3% x [728,000 - 8,000 + 180,000 shares] = 27,000 additional shares

Exercise 19-3 (concluded)

d. December 2 – declaration date

Retained earnings	7,600	
Cash dividends payable ($100,000 par x 7.6%)		7,600

December 19 – date of record

no entry

December 27 – payment date

Cash dividends payable	7,600	
Cash		7,600

e. December 2 – declaration date

Retained earnings	463,500	
Cash dividends payable (927,000* x $.50)		463,500

* 728,000 - 8,000 + 180,000 + 27,000 = 927,000 shares

December 19 – date of record

no entry

December 27 – payment date

Cash dividends payable	463,500	
Cash		463,500

Requirement 2

Paid-in capital:	
Preferred stock, 7.6%, 100,000 shares at $1 par	$ 100,000
Common stock, 927,000[1] shares at $1 par	927,000
Paid-in capital – excess of par, preferred	2,900,000
Paid-in capital – excess of par, common	5,275,000 [2]
Retained earnings	9,488,580 [3]
Treasury stock, at cost; 8,000 common shares	(88,000)
Total shareholders' equity	$18,402,580

[1] 728,000 - 8,000 + 180,000 + 27,000 = 927,000 shares

[2] $5,158,000 - 180,000 + 297,000 = $5,275,000

[3] $9,800,000 - 500,000 - 324,000 - 7,600 - 463,500 + 900,000 = $9,488,580

PROBLEMS

Problem 19-1

Requirement 1

a. March 6, 2000

($ in millions)

Par Value Method

Treasury stock (3 million sh. x $1)	3	
Paid-in capital – excess of par (3 million shares x $7*)	21	
Paid-in capital – reacquired shares	1	
Retained earnings (plug)	5	
Cash		30

* Paid-in capital – excess of par: $560 ÷ 80

Cost Method

Treasury stock (3 million sh. x $10)	30	
Cash		30

b. September 3, 2000

Par Value Method

Cash (1 million sh. x $11)	11	
Treasury stock (1 million sh. x $1)		1
Paid-in capital – excess of par		10

Cost Method

Cash (1 million sh. x $11)	11	
Treasury stock (1 million sh. x $10)		10
Paid-in capital– reacquired sh.		1

c. November 14, 2002

Par Value Method

Cash	14	
Treasury stock (2 million sh. x $1)		2
Paid-in capital – excess of par		12

Cost Method

Cash	14	
Paid-in cap.- reacquired sh.(1 +4)	5	
Retained earnings (plug)	1	
Treasury stock (2 million sh. x $10)		20

Problem 19-1 (concluded)

Requirement 2

Shareholders' Equity		$ in millions
	Par Value Method	**Cost Method**
Paid-in capital:		
Common stock, 80 million shares at $1 par, ...	$ 80	$ 80
Less: treasury stock, 1 million shares (at par)	(1)	
Paid-in capital – excess of par	561 *	560
Paid-in capital – reacquired shares................................	0	0
Retained earnings..	339 **	349 ***
Less: treasury stock, 1 million shares (at cost)		(10)
Total shareholders' equity..	$979	$979

* 560 - 21 + 10 + 12

** 350 - 11

*** 350 - 1

or, alternatively:

	Par Value Method	**Cost Method**
Paid-in capital:		
Common stock, 80 million shares at $1 par, ...	$ 80	$ 80
Less: treasury stock, 1 million shares (at par)	(1)	
Additional paid-in capital	561 *	560
Retained earnings..	339 **	349 ***
Less: treasury stock, 1 million shares (at cost)		(10)
Total shareholders' equity..	$979	$979

* 560 - 21 + 10 + 12

** 350 - 11

*** 350 - 1

Problem 19-2

Requirement 1

a. November 2 – declaration date

Retained earnings	252,000,000	
Cash dividends payable (315 million shares at $.80/share)		252,000,000

November 16 – date of record

no entry

December 2 – payment date

Cash dividends payable	252,000,000	
Cash		252,000,000

b. March 3 – declaration date

Investment in bonds	900,000	
Gain on appreciation of investment ($4.8 million – 3.9 million		900,000
Retained earnings	4,800,000	
Property dividends payable		4,800,000

March 14– date of record

no entry

April 6– payment date

Property dividends payable	4,800,000	
Investment in bonds		4,800,000

c. July 13

Retained earnings (15,750,000* x $21 per share)...........	330,750,000	
Common stock ([15,750,000* – 750,000] x $1 par) ...		15,000,000
Paid-in capital – excess of par ([15,750,000* – 750,000] x $20 per share)		300,000,000
Cash (750,000 shares at $21 market price per share).....		15,750,000

* 5% x 315,000,000 shares = 15,750,000 additional shares

Problem 19-2 (continued)

d. November 2 – declaration date

	Debit	Credit
Retained earnings	264,000,000	
Cash dividends payable (330,000,000* x $.80)		264,000,000

* 315,000,000 + 15,000,000 = 330,000,000 shares

November 16 – date of record

no entry

December 2 – payment date

	Debit	Credit
Cash dividends payable	264,000,000	
Cash		264,000,000

e. January 16

	Debit	Credit
Paid-in capital – excess of par	165,000,000	
Common stock (165,000,000* shares at $1 par)		165,000,000

* 330,000,000 shares x 50% = 165,000,000 shares

f. November 2 – declaration date

	Debit	Credit
Retained earnings	321,750,000	
Cash dividends payable (495,000,000 * x $.65)		321,750,000

* 315,000,000 + 15,000,000 + 165,000,000 = 495,000,000 shares

November 16 – date of record

no entry

December 2 – payment date

	Debit	Credit
Cash dividends payable	321,750,000	
Cash		321,750,000

Problem 19-2 (concluded)

Requirement 2

BLT Corporation
Statement of Shareholders' Equity
For the Years Ended Dec. 31, 2000, 2001, and 2002 ($ in 000s)

	Common Stock	Additional Paid-in Capital	Retained Earnings	Total Shareholders' Equity
Jan. 1, 2000	**315,000**	**1,890,000**	**2,910,000**	**5,115,000**
Net income			990,000	990,000
Cash dividends			(252,000)	(252,000)
Dec. 31, 2000	**315,000**	**1,890,000**	**3,648,000**	**5,853,000**
Property dividends			(4,800)	(4,800)
Common stock dividend	15,000	300,000	(330,750)	(15,750)
Net income			1,185,000	1,185,000
Cash dividends			(264,000)	(264,000)
Dec. 31, 2001	**330,000**	**2,190,000**	**4,233,450**	**6,753,450**
3 for 2 split effected in the form of a stock dividend	165,000	(165,000)		
Net income			1,365,000	1,365,000
Cash dividends			(321,750)	(321,750)
Dec. 31, 2002	**495,000**	**2,025,000**	**5,276,700**	**7,796,700**

Chapter 20 Earnings Per Share

EXERCISES

Exercise 20-1

1. EPS in 2000

(amounts in millions, except per share amount)

$$\frac{\overset{\text{net income}}{\$1{,}200}}{\underset{\text{shares at Jan. 1}}{606} \; - \underset{\text{treasury shares}}{18\,(^{10}/_{12})} \; + \underset{\text{treasury shares sold}}{18\,(^{2}/_{12})} \; + \underset{\text{new shares}}{72\,(^{1}/_{12})}} \qquad \frac{\$1{,}200}{600} = \underset{\text{Earnings Per Share}}{\$2.00}$$

2. EPS in 2001

(amounts in thousands, except per share amount)

$$\frac{\overset{\text{net income}}{\$1{,}200}}{\underset{\text{shares at Jan. 1}}{(606 - 18 + 18 + 72)} \; \underset{\text{stock dividend adjustment}}{\times (2.00)}} \qquad \frac{\$1{,}200}{1{,}356} = \underset{\text{Earnings Per Share}}{\$.88}$$

3. 2000 EPS in the 2001 comparative financial statements

(amounts in thousands, except per share amount)

$$\frac{\overset{\text{net income}}{\$1{,}200}}{\underset{\text{weighted average shares as previously calculated}}{600} \; \underset{\text{stock dividend adjustment}}{\times (2.00)}} \qquad \frac{\$1{,}200}{1{,}200} = \underset{\text{Earnings Per Share}}{\$1.00}$$

PROBLEMS

Problem 20-1

1. Net loss per share for the year ended December 31, 2000:

(amounts in millions, except per share amount)

$$\frac{\underset{\text{net loss}}{-\$280} \quad \underset{\text{preferred dividends}}{-\$280^{1}}}{\underset{\text{shares at Jan. 1}}{1{,}200\,(1.05)} \; \underset{\text{treasury shares}}{-\,60\,(8/12)}\;(1.05) \quad \underset{\text{new shares}}{+\,24\,(4/12)}} = \frac{-\$560}{1{,}226} = (\$.46) \text{ Net Loss Per Share}$$

(1.05): stock dividend adjustment

2. Per share amount of income or loss from continuing operations for the year ended December 31, 2000:

(amounts in millions, except per share amount)

$$\frac{\underset{\text{operating income}}{\$520^{2}} \quad \underset{\text{preferred dividends}}{-\$280^{1}}}{\underset{\text{shares at Jan. 1}}{1{,}200(1.05)} \; \underset{\text{treasury shares}}{-\,60\,(8/12)}\;(1.05) \quad \underset{\text{new shares}}{+\,24\,(4/12)}} = \frac{\$240}{1{,}226} = \$.19 \text{ Income from Continuing Operations Per Share}$$

(1.05): stock dividend adjustment

[1] 40,000 shares x \$100 x 7% = \$280,000

[2] \$800,000 – \$280,000 = \$520,000

Problem 20-1 (concluded)

3. 2000 and 1999 comparative income statements:

(amounts in millions, except per share amount)

	2000	1999
Earnings (Loss) Per Common Share:		
Income (loss) from operations before extraordinary items	$ .19	$.71
Extraordinary loss from litigation settlement	(.65)	—
Net income (loss)	($ .46)	$.71

Note: The weighted average number of common shares in 1999 should be adjusted for the stock dividend in 2000 for the purpose of reporting 1999 EPS in subsequent years for comparative purposes:

$$\frac{\underset{\text{net income}}{\$900}}{\underset{\text{shares at Jan. 1}}{1{,}200} \quad \underset{\text{stock dividend adjustment}}{(1.05)}} = \frac{\$900}{1{,}260} = \underset{\text{Earnings Per Share}}{\$.71}$$

Problem 20-2

(amounts in millions, except per share amount)

$$\frac{\underset{\text{net income}}{\$1,050} \quad \underset{\text{preferred dividends}}{-\$39}}{\underset{\text{shares at Jan. 1}}{300(1.04)} + \underset{\text{new shares}}{30\,(^{10}/_{12})}\ (1.04) - \underset{\text{shares retired}}{2\,(^{6}/_{12})}} = \frac{\$1,011}{337} = \$3.00$$

↑ stock dividend adjustment ↑ (applies to the 1.04 factors)

Problem 20-3

The options issued in 1998 are not considered when calculating 2000 EPS because the exercise price ($34) is not less than the 2000 average market price of $32 (although they would have been considered when calculating 1998 or 1999 EPS if the average price those years had been more than $34).

The options issued in 2000 do not affect the calculation of 2000 EPS because they were issued at December 31. Options are assumed exercised at the beginning of the year or when granted, whichever is later — when granted, in this case. So, the fraction of the year the shares are assumed outstanding is $^{0}/_{12}$, meaning no increase in the weighted average shares.

The options issued in 1999 are considered exercised for 4 million shares when calculating 2000 EPS because the exercise price ($24) is less than the 2000 average market price of $32. Treasury shares are assumed repurchased at the average price for diluted EPS:

	4 million shares	
x	$24	(exercise price)
	$96 million	
÷	$32	(average market price)
	3 million shares	

Problem 20-3 (concluded)

(amounts in millions, except per share amounts)

Basic EPS

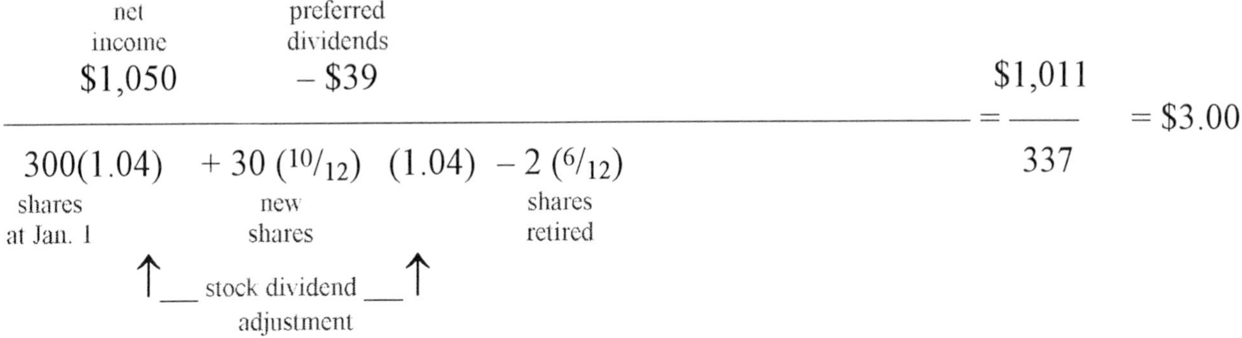

Diluted EPS

$$\frac{\underset{\text{net income}}{\$1{,}050} \; \underset{\text{preferred dividends}}{- \$39} \; \underset{\text{after-tax interest savings}}{+ \$40 - 40\%(\$40)}}{\underset{\text{shares at Jan. 1}}{300(1.04)} + \underset{\text{new shares}}{30\,(^{10}/_{12})}\,(1.04) - \underset{\text{shares retired}}{2\,(^{6}/_{12})} + \underset{\text{exercise of options}}{(4-3)} + \underset{\text{contingent shares}}{13^{*}} + \underset{\text{conversion of bonds}}{12^{**}}} = \frac{\$1{,}035}{363} = \$2.85$$

(↑ stock dividend adjustment ↑ — the (1.04) factors applied to shares at Jan. 1 and new shares)

* The contingently issuable shares are considered issued when calculating diluted EPS because the condition for issuance (RW net income > $250 million) currently is being met.

** The bonds are considered converted when calculating diluted EPS: 400,000 bonds x 30 shares = 12 million shares upon conversion. Interest = $400 million x 10% = $40 million.

Problem 20-4

(amounts in millions, except per share amounts)

Basic EPS

$$\frac{\underset{\text{net income}}{\$1,300} \quad \underset{\text{preferred dividends}}{-\ \$80^*}}{\underset{\text{shares at Jan. 1}}{880} \quad \underset{\text{new shares}}{+\ 32\ (3/12)}} = \frac{\$1,220}{888} = \$1.37$$

Diluted EPS

$$\frac{\underset{\text{net income}}{\$1,300} \quad \underset{\text{preferred dividends}}{-\ \$80^*} \quad \underset{\text{preferred dividends}}{+\ 80^*}}{\underset{\text{shares at Jan. 1}}{880} \quad \underset{\text{new shares}}{+\ 32\ (3/12)} \quad \underset{\text{exercise of options}}{+\ (40 - 30^{**})} \quad \underset{\text{conversion of preferred shares}}{+\ 80}} = \frac{\$1,300}{978} = \$1.33$$

* 8 million shares x $100 par x 10% = $80 million

****Assumed purchase of treasury shares**

	40 million shares	
x	$30	(exercise price)
	$1,200 million	
÷	$40	(average market price)
	30 million shares	

Chapter 21 Accounting Changes and Error Corrections

EXERCISES

Exercise 21-1

Cumulative effect:

SYD depreciation		*SL depreciation*		
$\left(\frac{10+9+8}{55} \times [\$105,000 - 6,000]\right)$	–	$(^3/_{10} \times [\$105,000 - 6,000])$	=	
\$48,600	–	\$29,700	=	\$18,900

Accumulated depreciation	18,900	
Cumulative effect of accounting change		18,900

Adjusting entry (2000 depreciation):

Depreciation expense (\$99,000 ÷ 10 years)	9,900	
Accumulated depreciation		9,900

Exercise 21-2

Requirement 1

To record the change:

Cumulative effect of accounting change	24,600	
Inventory (\$96,000 – 71,400)		24,600

Requirement 2

The cumulative income effect is reported as a separate item of income between extraordinary items and net income. The effect of the change on certain key income numbers should be disclosed for the current period and on a "pro forma" basis for the financial statements of all prior periods that are included for comparison with the current financial statements. Also, the nature of and justification for the change should be described in the disclosure notes.

Exercise 21-3

Requirement 1

Accrued liability and expense		
Warranty expense (4% x $720,000)	28,800	
Estimated warranty liability		28,800
Actual expenditures (summary entry)		
Estimated warranty liability	17,600	
Cash, wages payable, parts and supplies, etc.		17,600

Requirement 2

Actual expenditures (summary entry)		
Estimated warranty liability ($15,000 – $4,600)	10,400	
Loss on product warranty (4% – 3%] x $500,000)	5,000	
Cash, wages payable, parts and supplies, etc.		15,400*

*(4% x $500,000) – $4,600 = $10,400

PROBLEMS

Problem 21-1

a. This is a change in estimate.

No entry is needed to record the change		
2000 adjusting entry:		
Warranty expense (3% x $800,000)	24,000	
Estimated warranty liability		24,000

A disclosure note should describe the effect of a change in estimate on income before extraordinary items, net income, and related per-share amounts for the current period.

b. This is a change in estimate.

No entry is needed to record the change		
2000 adjusting entry:		
Depreciation expense (determined below)	112,500	
Accumulated depreciation		112,500

Calculation of annual depreciation after the estimate change:

	$4,000,000	Cost
$100,000		Old depreciation ($4,000,000 ÷ 40 years)
x 3 yrs	(300,000)	Depreciation to date (1997-1999)
	$ 3,700,000	Undepreciated cost
	(2,800,000)	New estimated salvage value
	$ 900,000	To be depreciated
	÷ 8	Estimated remaining life (8 years: 2000-2007)
	$ 112,500	New annual depreciation

A disclosure note should describe the effect of a change in estimate on income before extraordinary items, net income, and related per-share amounts for the current period.

Problem 21-1 (continued)

c. This is a change in accounting principle that is reported prospectively.

No entry is needed to record the change.

When a company changes ***to*** *the LIFO inventory method* from another inventory method, accounting records usually are insufficient to determine the cumulative income effect of the change or to determine pro forma disclosures for prior years. So, a company changing to LIFO does not report the cumulative income effect in current income nor revise the balance in retained earnings. Instead, the base year inventory for all future LIFO calculations is the beginning inventory in the year the LIFO method is adopted ($13 million in this case). The only disclosure required is a footnote to the financial statements describing the nature of and justification for the change as well as an explanation as to why the cumulative income effect was omitted.

d. This is a change in accounting principle.

To record the change:

Accumulated depreciation (determined below)	216,000	
Deferred tax liability ($216,000 x 40%)		86,400
Cumulative effect of accounting change (net effect)		129,600

***Cumulative effect of the change:** ($ in 000s)

	SYD		Straight-line	
1996 depreciation	$180	($990 x 10/55)	$99	($990 ÷ 10)
1997 depreciation	162	($990 x 9/55)	99	($990 ÷ 10)
1998 depreciation	144	($990 x 8/55)	99	($990 ÷ 10)
1999 depreciation	126	($990 x 7/55)	99	($990 ÷ 10)
Accumulated depreciation and 1996-99 reduction in income	$612	▼ difference $216	$396	

2000 adjusting entry:

Depreciation expense ($990,000 ÷ 10 years)	99,000	
Accumulated depreciation		99,000

Problem 21-1 (concluded)

Tax depreciation (MACRS) would have been more than SYD depreciation during the four previous years, but the temporary difference would have been still more if accounting income had been based on straight-line depreciation. As a result, the deferred tax liability is increased from what it was to what it would have been if straight-line depreciation had been used the four previous years. It's not necessary to know what the old or new balance is – only that the new balance should be $86,400 higher.

The cumulative income effect is reported as a separate item of income between extraordinary items and net income. The effect of the change on certain key income numbers should be disclosed for the current period and on a "pro forma" basis for the financial statements of all prior periods that are included for comparison with the current financial statements. Also, the nature of and justification for the change should be described in the disclosure notes.

e. This is a change in estimate.

To revise the liability on the basis of the new estimate:

Loss – litigation	5,000,000	
Liability - litigation ($45 million – 40 million)		5,000,000

A disclosure note should describe the effect of a change in estimate on income before extraordinary items, net income, and related per-share amounts for the current period.

f. This is a change in accounting principle.

Because the change will be effective only for assets placed in service after the date of change, there would be no cumulative effect on prior years' earnings because the change doesn't affect assets depreciated in prior periods.

The nature of and justification for the change should be described in the disclosure notes. Also, the effect of the change on the current period's income before extraordinary items, net income, and related per-share amounts should be disclosed.

Problem 21-2

a. To correct the error:

Equipment (cost)	9,000	
Accumulated depreciation ([$9,000 ÷ 5] x 2 years))		3,600
Retained earnings ($9,000 – [$1,800 x 2 years))		5,400

2000 adjusting entry:

Depreciation expense ($9,000 ÷ 5)	1,800	
Accumulated depreciation		1,800

b. To reverse erroneous entry:

Cash	51,000	
Office supplies		51,000

To record correct entry:

Storage boxes	51,000	
Cash		51,000

c. To correct the error:

Inventory	112,000	
Retained earnings		112,000

d. To correct the error:

Retained earnings ([$10 x 4,000 shares] – $4,000)	36,000	
Paid-in capital – excess of par		36,000

Note: A "small" stock dividend (<25%) requires that the market value of the additional shares be "capitalized.".

e. To correct the error:

Retained earnings (overstatement of 1999 income)	120,000	
Interest expense (overstatement of 2000 interest)		120,000

2000 adjusting entry:

Interest expense (4/6 x $180,000)	120,000	
Interest payable (4/6 x $180,000)		120,000

f. To correct the error:

Prepaid insurance ($216,000 ÷ 3 yrs x 2 years: 2000-2001)	144,000	
Retained earnings ($216,000 – [$216,000 ÷ 3 years])		144,000

2000 adjusting entry:

Insurance expense ($216,000 ÷ 3 years)	72,000	
Prepaid insurance		72,000

Chapter 22 The Statement of Cash Flows Revisited

EXERCISES

Exercise 22-1

Situation	Cost of goods sold	Inventory	Accounts payable increase (decrease)	Cash paid to suppliers increase (decrease)
1	600	0	0	**600**

1. Spreadsheet Entry	Cost of goods sold	600	
	Cash (paid to suppliers of goods)		**600**

Situation	Cost of goods sold	Inventory	Accounts payable	Cash paid to suppliers
2	600	18	0	**618**

2. Spreadsheet Entry	Cost of goods sold	600	
	Inventory	18	
	Cash (paid to suppliers of goods)		**618**

Situation	Cost of goods sold	Inventory	Accounts payable	Cash paid to suppliers
3	600	0	558	**558**

3. Spreadsheet Entry	Cost of goods sold	600	
	Accounts payable		42
	Cash (paid to suppliers of goods)		**558**

Situation	Cost of goods sold	Inventory	Accounts payable	Cash paid to suppliers
4	600	18	42	**576**

4. Spreadsheet Entry	Cost of goods sold	600	
	Inventory	18	
	Accounts payable		42
	Cash (paid to suppliers of goods)		**576**

Situation	Cost of goods sold	Inventory	Accounts payable	Cash paid to suppliers
5	600	(18)	(42)	**624**

5. Spreadsheet Entry	Cost of goods sold	600	
	Accounts payable	42	
	Inventory		18
	Cash (paid to suppliers of goods)		**624**

Exercise 22-2

RECONCILIATION OF NET INCOME TO NET CASH FLOWS FROM OPERATING ACTIVITIES

	($ in millions)
Net income	$ 78
***Adjustments for noncash effects*:**	
Increase in accounts receivable	(162)
Increase (decrease) in inventory	0
Increase in accounts payable	29
Increase in salaries payable	12
Decrease in prepaid insurance	18
Depreciation expense	33
Depletion expense	15
Decrease in bond discount	3
Gain on sale of equipment	(75)
Loss on sale of land	24
Increase in income tax payable	36
Net cash flows from operating activities	$ 21

Exercise 22-3

Requirement 1:

a. Spreadsheet Entry	Cash (received from customers)	**933**	
	Accounts receivable		18
	Sales revenue		915

b. Spreadsheet Entry	Cost of goods sold	555	
	Inventory	39	
	Accounts payable	24	
	Cash (paid to suppliers of goods)		**618**

c. Spreadsheet Entry	Salaries expense	123	
	Salaries payable		15
	Cash (paid to employees)		**108**

d. Spreadsheet Entry	Insurance expense	57	
	Prepaid insurance		27
	Cash (paid for insurance)		**30**

e. Spreadsheet Entry	Income tax expense	66	
	Income tax payable		60
	Cash (paid for income taxes)		**6**

Depreciation expense and the loss on sale of land are not cash outflows.

Requirement 2:

Cash Flows from Operating Activities:	
Cash received from customers	$933
Cash paid to suppliers	(618)
Cash paid to employees	(108)
Cash paid for insurance	(30)
Cash paid for income taxes	(6)
Net cash flows from operating activities	$171

Exercise 22-4

RECONCILIATION OF NET INCOME TO NET CASH FLOWS FROM OPERATING ACTIVITIES

Net loss	$ (25,000)
***Adjustments for noncash effects*:**	
Depreciation expense	30,000
Increase in salaries payable	2,500
Decrease in accounts receivable	10,000
Increase in inventory	(11,500)
Amortization of patent	1,500
Reduction in discount on bonds	1,000
Net cash flows from operating activities	$8,500

PROBLEMS

Problem 22-1

Classifications

+ I	Investing activity (cash inflow)
– I	Investing activity (cash outflow
+ F	Financing activity (cash inflow)
– F	Financing activity (cash outflow)
N	Noncash investing and financing activity
X	Not reported as an investing and/or a financing activity

Transactions

Example __+ I__ 1. Sale of a building
__+F__ 2. Issuance of preferred stock for cash
__- F__ 3. Retirement of preferred stock
__N__ 4. Conversion of bonds to common stock
__N__ 5. Lease of a machine by capital lease
__+ I__ 6. Sale of a trademark
__- I__ 7. Purchase of land for cash
__N__ 8. Issuance of common stock for a building
__+ I__ 9. Collection of a note receivable (principal amount)
__+F__ 10. Sale of bonds payable
__X__ 11. Distribution of a stock dividend
__N__ 12. Payment of property dividend
__- F__ 13. Payment of cash dividends
__+F__ 14. Issuance of a short-term note payable for cash
__+F__ 15. Issuance of a long-term note payable for cash
__- I__ 16. Purchase of investment securities (not cash equivalent)
__- F__ 17. Repayment of a note payable
__X__ 18. Cash payment for 3-year insurance policy
__+ I__ 19. Sale of land
__N__ 20. Issuance of note payable for land
__- I__ 21. Purchase of common stock issued by another corporation
__N__ 22. Repayment of long-term debt by issuing common stock
__X__ 23. Restriction of retained earnings for plant expansion
__X__ 24. Payment of semiannual interest on notes payable
__- F__ 25. Purchase of treasury stock
__- I__ 26. Loan to a subsidiary
__X__ 27. Sale of merchandise to customers
__X__ 28. Purchase of treasury bills (cash equivalents)

Problem 22-2

A2Z Industries

Spreadsheet for the Statement of Cash Flows

	Dec.31 1999	Changes Debits	Credits	Dec. 31 2000
Balance Sheet				
Assets:				
Cash	1,125	(14) 675		1,800
Accounts receivable	1,350	(1) 450		1,800
Inventory	1,575	(4)1,125		2,700
Land	1,800	(2) 450 x	(3) 225	2,025
Building	2,700			2,700
Less: Acc. depreciation	(810)		(5) 90	(900)
Equipment	6,750	(11)2,700	(7) 900	8,550
Less: Acc. depreciation	(1,440)	(7) 810	(6) 945	(1,575)
Goodwill	4,500		(8) 900	3,600
	17,550			20,700
Liabilities:				
Accounts payable	1,350		(4) 900	2,250
Accrued expenses	675		(9) 225	900
Lease liability – land	0		x (2) 450	450
Shareholders' Equity:				
Common stock	9,000		(12) 450	9,450
Paid-in capital-ex. of par	2,025		(12) 225	2,250
Retained earnings	4,500	(12) 675	(10)2,925	
		(13)1,350		5,400
	17,550			20,700
Income Statement				
Revenues:				
Sales revenue			(1)7,935	7,935
Gain on sale of land			(3) 270	270
Expenses:				
Cost of goods sold		(4)1,800		1,800
Depreciation expense-build.		(5) 90		90
Depreciation expense-equip.		(6) 945		945
Loss on sale of equipment		(7) 45		45
Amortization of goodwill		(8) 900		900
Operating expenses		(9) 1,500		1,500
Net income		**(10)2,925**		**2,925**

Problem 22-2 (continued)

Spreadsheet for the Statement of Cash Flows
(continued)

	Dec. 31 1999	Changes Debits	Changes Credits	Dec. 31 2000
Statement of Cash Flows				
Operating activities:				
Cash inflows:				
From customers		(1)7,485		
Cash outflows:				
To suppliers of goods			(4)2,025	
For operating expenses			(9)1,275	
Net cash flows				4,185
Investing activities:				
Purchase of equipment			(11)2,700	
Sale of land		(3) 495		
Sale of equipment		(7) 45		
Net cash flows				(2,160)
Financing activities:				
Payment of cash dividends			(13)1,350	
Net cash flows				(1,350)
Net increase in cash			(14) 675	675
Totals		**24,465**	**24,465**	

✗ Noncash investing and financing activity

Problem 22-2 (concluded)

A2Z Industries
Statement of Cash Flows
For year ended December 31, 2000 ($ in 000)

Cash flows from operating activities:		
Cash inflows:		
From customers	$7,485	
Cash outflows:		
To suppliers of goods	(2,025)	
For operating expenses	(1,275)	
Net cash flows from operating activities		$4,185
Cash flows from investing activities:		
Purchase of equipment	$ (2,700)	
Sale of land	495	
Sale of equipment	45	
Net cash flows from investing activities		(2,160)
Cash flows from financing activities:		
Payment of cash dividends	$ (1,350)	
Net cash flows from financing activities		(1,350)
Net increase in cash		$ 675
Cash balance, January 1		1,125
Cash balance, December 31		$1,800
Noncash investing and financing activities:		
Land acquired by capital lease		$450

Problem 22-3

A2Z Industries

Spreadsheet for the Statement of Cash Flows

	Dec.31 1999	Changes Debits	Changes Credits	Dec. 31 2000
Balance Sheet				
Assets:				
Cash	1,125	(15) 675		1,800
Accounts receivable	1,350	(7) 450		1,800
Inventory	1,575	(8)1,125		2,700
Land	1,800	(11) 450 ✗	(2) 225	2,025
Building	2,700			2,700
Less: Acc. depreciation	(810)		(3) 90	(900)
Equipment	6,750	(12)2,700	(5) 900	8,550
Less: Acc. depreciation	(1,440)	(5) 810	(4) 945	(1,575)
Goodwill	4,500		(6) 900	3,600
	17,550			20,700
Liabilities:				
Accounts payable	1,350		(9) 900	2,250
Accrued expenses	675		(10) 225	900
Lease liability–land	0		✗ (11) 450	450
Shareholders' Equity:				
Common stock	9,000		(13) 450	9,450
Paid-in capital-ex. of par	2,025		(13) 225	2,250
Retained earnings	4,500	(13) 675	(1)2,925	
		(14)1,350		5,400
	17,550			20,700

✗ Noncash investing and financing activity

Problem 22-3 (continued)

Spreadsheet for the Statement of Cash Flows
(continued)

	Dec.31 1999	Changes Debits	Changes Credits	Dec. 31 2000
Statement of Cash Flows				
Operating activities:				
Net income		(1)2,925		
Adjustments for noncash effects:				
Gain on sale of land			(2) 270	
Depreciation expense-build		(3) 90		
Depreciation expense-equip		(4) 945		
Loss on sale of equipment		(5) 45		
Amortization of goodwill		(6) 900		
Increase in accounts receivable			(7) 450	
Increase in inventory			(8)1,125	
Increase in accounts payable		(9) 900		
Increase in accrued expenses		(10) 225		
Net cash flows				4,185
Investing activities:				
Purchase of equipment			(12)2,700	
Sale of land		(2) 495		
Sale of equipment		(5) 45		
Net cash flows				(2,160)
Financing activities:				
Payment of cash dividends			(14)1,350	
Net cash flows				(1,350)
Net increase in cash			(15) 675	675
Totals		**14,805**	**14,805**	

Problem 22-3 (concluded)

A2Z Industries
Statement of Cash Flows
For year ended December 31, 2000 ($ in 000)

Cash flows from operating activities:		
Net income	$ 2,925	
Adjustments for noncash effects:		
Gain on sale of land	(270)	
Depreciation expense – building	90	
Depreciation expense – equipment	945	
Loss on sale of equipment	45	
Amortization of goodwill	900	
Increase in accounts receivable	(450)	
Increase in inventory	(1,125)	
Increase in accounts payable	900	
Increase in accrued expenses	225	
Net cash flows from operating activities		$4,185
Cash flows from investing activities:		
Purchase of equipment	$(2,700)	
Sale of land	495	
Sale of equipment	45	
Net cash flows from investing activities		(2,160)
Cash flows from financing activities:		
Payment of cash dividends	$(1,350)	
Net cash flows from financing activities		(1,350)
Net increase in cash		$ 675
Cash balance, January 1		1,125
Cash balance, December 31		$1,800
Noncash investing and financing activities:		
Land acquired by capital lease		$450